25 MANAGEMENT TECHNIQUES
IN 90 MINUTES

For a complete list of Management Books 2000 titles, visit our website on www.mb2000.com

The original idea for the 'In Ninety Minutes' series was presented to the publishers by Graham Willmott, author of 'Forget Debt in Ninety Minutes'. Thanks are due to him for suggesting what has become a major series to help business people, entrepreneurs, managers, supervisors and others to greatly improve their personal performance, after just a short period of study.

Proposed titles in the 'in Ninety Minutes' series are:

Forget Debt in Ninety Minutes
Understand Accounts in Ninety Minutes
Working Together in Ninety Minutes
Supply Chain in Ninety Minutes
Networking in Ninety Minutes
25 Management Techniques in Ninety Minutes
Practical Negotiating in Ninety Minutes
Find That Job in Ninety Minutes
Control Credit in Ninety Minutes
Faster Promotions in Ninety Minutes
Managing Your Boss in Ninety Minutes
Better Budgeting in Ninety Minutes
... other titles may be added

The series editor is James Alexander

Submissions of possible titles for this series or for management books in general will be welcome. MB2000 are always keen to discuss possible new works that might be added to their extensive list of books for people who mean business.

25 MANAGEMENT TECHNIQUES in 90 Minutes

Byron Kalies

2000

First published in 2005 by Management Books 2000 Ltd
Forge House, Limes Road
Kemble, Cirencester
Gloucestershire, GL7 6AD, UK
Tel: 0044 (0) 1285 771441
Fax: 0044 (0) 1285 771055
E-mail: mb2000@btconnect.com
Web: www.mb2000.com

Printed and bound in Great Britain by Digital Books Logistics Ltd of Peterborough

British Library Cataloguing in Publication Data is available

ISBN 1-85252-480-4

Contents

<table>
<tr><td>

TECHNIQUE NO 1

</td><td>

Real Time Management
or ... How Would You Like to Be Remembered?

</td></tr>
</table>

> *'What is this life if, full of care,*
> *We have no time to stand and stare.'*
>
> W H Davies

Time management training is awful. Time logging, hints for dealing with telephone calls, email tips – nothing seems to work. You can't even begin to look at taking anything away from a time management course until you've considered your own mortality.

Try this exercise

> It's ten years in the future. You find yourself in a church at your own funeral. One by one, people you know get up and talk about you and your contribution to the world. What are they going to say? What will your partner, your kids, your colleagues say? I can bet all the money in my pocket they won't be wishing you'd spent just a few more hours in work at your desk.

So, having come to terms with your mortality what next? Next you look at the scenario slightly differently. How would you like to be remembered? What would you like those who care about you, and you care about, to say? That'll be your starter. Once you've really got this big picture sorted you can move on.

The next exercise comes from Stephen Covey. It's linked to the previous exercise and is known as 'Stephen Covey's Big Rocks'. Imagine a bucket. Put three or four big rocks in.

'Is the bucket full?'

'No,' you reply.

'Of course not,' I say and put some smaller rocks in it to fill in the gaps.

'Is it full now?'

'No.'

I put in some sand, then some water. It's full. (Okay, I know you could add some gas, but we'll assume it's full).

So, what's the learning here? It's to do with the order. What would happen if you'd reversed the order? Put the water in first, then the sand, the small rocks. There would be no room for the big rocks. These big rocks are the important things in your life. You need to schedule them first, not try to squeeze them in after arranging the water (writing pointless assessments), sand (unnecessary travel) or small rocks (staff meetings where no-one listens and everyone keeps looking at the clock). What are the big rocks in your life? For many, it's things like family, time to watch the children grow up, time to write that novel, time for themselves, time to make a difference. You decide. You identify three or four things you believe are important, the three or four things that will make a difference at your funeral. When you've decided what they are, then schedule them. Schedule time for yourself, time to take that French class, time to watch the youngest's first sports day. Once these times are scheduled fit the rest of your work around them. Try it – it works.

It's not big and it's not clever to work more than forty hours a week. I repeat, it's not big and it's not clever. So stop it. Stop that 'poor me, look how many hours I work' nonsense. Work as little as you can. Do as much as you can in the time agreed, but once you've done – run away – go home. The surprise will be that people will hardly miss you at all. It may be hard at first to realise the world of work can carry on without you but give it time. This feeling will be replaced by one of immense joy. 'I'm dispensable!' This will give you enormous freedom.

There are ways of accelerating this process. Get a team of happy people to work for you. Build a group of people who appreciate and trust you. One of the great ways of building up this trust and appreciation turns old time management theory on its head. When you arrive at work, don't get straight to your desk and start wading through emails. When you arrive at work, talk to each member of your team, properly. Ask about his or her family, the son's football match, the health of the car, the cat or whatever is important to them. Invest the time in people – it really pays dividends in the long run.

Once you've got all this sorted, time management is a piece of cake. There are useful little tips about only opening emails twice a day that you can totally ignore. Why? Because you're a human being and incredibly curious. Think of the Pareto principle. This states that 20% of effort gives you 80% of the result. This is excellent. Unless there is a dire need to complete everything (carrying out a heart transplant would fit into this category), ask yourself if you could live with getting 80%. If you can – perfect. You can then do something else and get the 80% of that from 20% of the effort.

There are lots of hints and tips about time logs, to-do lists, telephones, meetings, emails, mails, procrastination, 'time stealers' (a philosophically difficult concept for me to get my head around), paperwork and working from home. Have a look at each one. Then discount 80% of them. If you've heard of them but are still not doing them, my guess is you never will. If they are new and sound interesting – try them.

But never forget the big picture. Why save ten minutes in handling paperwork if you're only going to spend it trawling through useless emails. Remember you can't save time – you've only got so much. You know that.

So now – what do you want to be remembered for?

<table>
<tr><td>

**TECHNIQUE
NO 2**

</td><td>

Learning, Trust and Making Mistakes

</td></tr>
</table>

'The only competitive advantage the company of the future will have is its managers' ability to learn faster than their competitors.'

Arie de Geus

There's the story about a top salesman in the aircraft industry who messed up. He lost a $5,000,000 contract. At his desk the next morning he starts going through his papers – tidying them up, clearing his desk. He gets a phone call from his manager,

'Have you got five minutes?'

'Sure,' he mumbles and slowly makes his way up the stairs to his boss' office.

As he enters the room he says, *'Look – I know I got it wrong – I'm sorry – I've written my letter of resignation – here it is,'* and he puts it on the desk.

His manager looks at the letter, rips it in half, rips it in half again and puts it in the bin.

'You must be joking,' she says smiling *'We've just spent $5,000,000 on your training – there's no way you're leaving until you've made that back for us.'*

Is this the way you and your Organisation deal with mistakes? It should be. If you don't then you're helping to create an environment of dishonesty, low risk taking and blame.

For example, I used to work as a computer programmer in an organisation that 'didn't tolerate mistakes'. One day, I incorrectly printed out 2.4 million address labels. For hours, the messengers delivered these labels to me. They were piling up in the corner, then taking over the whole room, gradually moving toward me. Luckily (!) my manager never came in my room – ever. Everything was communicated by email. So what do you think I did? Did I say, 'Hey

– sorry, I got it wrong – let's hire a truck and recycle this paper'? I did not. I was putting a few hundred of these in the waste bin every day. It took months of effort for me to get rid of them all. Not really the most cost effective use of my time.

As a manager, you know that people will make mistakes. You know that – don't you? Really! You also know that the biggest learning comes from the biggest mistakes. Think of the biggest learning experience you've had – something memorable. I would bet all the money in my pocket that it's not some wonderful experience when things worked beautifully. For me, it's the time I crashed the car. I'll never forget that experience. It was 12 years ago, but to this day, I always look right extremely carefully when turning left at a junction.

You have to allow people to take a 'big swing' as Jack Welch calls it. He tells the story of the new Halarc light bulb he helped develop in the late 1970s. It cost $50 million but no one wanted to pay $10.95 for a single light bulb, so it was shelved. Instead of punishing, or ignoring the staff who were involved, they received cash management rewards and several promotions for their efforts. They celebrated a great try rather than punishing a big failure.

So, if you really, truly want your staff to be creative, motivated and happy – tell them you want them to make mistakes. Tell them you'll punish them if they don't. Give them targets of how many mistakes they must make in a week and if they make more – give them a bonus. Trust them.

Some of the greatest products have come from mistakes: the original post-it note from 3M was made from a batch of glue that didn't stick, so a different use was made of it. Legend has it that it was used to mark the pages of the bible without damaging the pages. Play-Doh was originally designed as a wallpaper cleaner by Joe McVicker but was used by his sister's pre-school class as modelling clay.

But it's vital that when people make mistakes, you deal with it as an adult. Look at what happened, calmly. Find out what went wrong, non-blamefully. Make sure everyone learns from it and that the same mistake doesn't happen again.

It does all depend on the attitude you instil in your team toward taking risks and making mistakes. It took Thomas Edison 10,000 attempts to discover the correct combination of materials for the light bulb. Half way through the process a reporter asked him how he could keep going after failing 5,000 times. 'I haven't failed 5,000 times', he replied, 'I've successfully discovered 5,000 ways that don't work.'

Learning by definition – my definition at least – involves change. Otherwise why bother. This could be a change in attitude, behaviour, whatever, but at some level, a change.

At an organisational level, businesses need to change to survive. Reg Revons' formula for an organisation to survive ...

$$L > C$$

... (where L is the rate of learning and C is the rate of change) is even more true today where the rate of change increases almost week by week. Organisations that don't change die.

A great example of this working well happened in February 2000. Ford gave all their employees free computers and bargain Internet access. CEO Jacques Nasser wanted to ensure that the staff *'every one of us – is connected to what's going on in the marketplace so that we know where consumers are heading.'*

On the downside, Encyclopaedia Britannica was once a thriving world-wide organisation. In 1990 sales were $650 million. Then the CD-ROM came along. They resisted. 'It's a fad. People will always want to read our books' seemed to be their message. In May 1995 the company was put up for sale. No one wanted them. They were finally sold 18 months later for less than half the book value.

Success stories are from organisations that change and develop, take risks, make mistakes. Minnesota Mining and Manufacturing company started in 1902 mining for material for sandpaper. For the next 100 years they changed and developed – huge successes and huge failures – sandpaper, masking tape, magnetic tape, high tech products, everything now we associate with 3M.

Wells Fargo began 150 years ago as a stagecoach and messenger service and since then they've moved into insurance, banking and Internet banking with assets of over $300 billion.

Similarly, Hewlett Packard keep moving on by innovating. More than half of their company's current orders come from products that did not exist two years ago.

Successful organisations change and develop when things are working nicely as well as when things aren't going so good. They reward enterprise. They value mistakes. The Yamaha motor Company held an exhibition on products that hadn't worked ('First Yamaha Challenge Exhibition'). Pride of place went to the $833,000 super car from 1982 that was never sold.

Show off your mistakes, evaluate them, laugh about them – then move on. I would disagree with the traditional, nicely smooth learning curve (black dotted line) shown below.

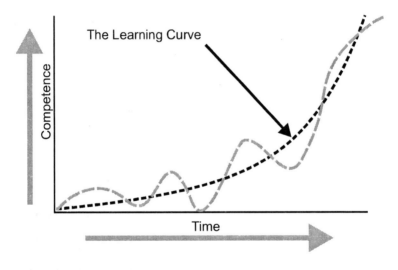

For me, life is more like the grey, wavy line – big failures followed by great learning and bigger successes. Take pride in your failure.

If your staff do everything they can to succeed but fail – reward them. If they genuinely cock-up because they've tried too hard praise them.

If your people knock on your door and say, *'Guess what? I've just lost a contract because I really went with my gut reaction but got it wrong,'* put your arm around their shoulder, not their neck. You know the next time they'll be even keener to get it right. You know that, don't you? Trust them.

<table>
<tr><td>TECHNIQUE NO 3</td><td>Telling The Truth and Equality of Opportunities</td></tr>
</table>

'You want the truth? You couldn't handle the truth!'

J Nicholson

The older I get, the easier (some parts of) my life get.

A simple phrase I picked up on a training course a few years ago has solved so many problems. You don't believe me? Try it. Run the experiment;

'When in doubt, tell the truth. When not in doubt, tell the truth.'

Simple. Easy. Brilliant. It works in all situations, at all times.

I was told that power comes from two sources:

There's positional power – power we give to people because of their relative social, economic, politic or cultural situation and then there's the power people earn from telling the truth. The best way to demonstrate that is to start doing it.

Use it as the staple answer for so many managerial problems and concerns. You're a manager so you have staff. So you have problems. It goes with the territory. Don't be surprised. It's like doctors complaining that they only get to meet sick people – it's going to happen. Get over it. Your staff have problems and they want you to help. More often than not their problem is you. Thankfully this works for those problems as well.

On a typical management training course:

'What do I do if my boss keeps interrupting me and I can't get my work done?' asks a course member.

'Tell her, "You keep interrupting me and I can't get my work done."'

'But I feel really awkward about telling her – she is my boss.'

'Tell her, "I feel really awkward about this as you're my boss but

you keep interrupting me and I can't get my work done."'
'But ...'
'What do you think will happen?'
'Probably nothing.'
'What's the worse thing that could possibly happen?'
'I'd get sacked.'
'Well you hate the job anyway ... I'm joking. You won't get sacked
for telling the truth, will you? Trust me – I'm a trainer.'

A few days later I had a phone call from the course member.

'I did it. She never had the faintest idea that it was annoying me.
She thought I looked lonely and came to chat to me.'

It really can be that simple. It frequently is.

The first time I ran this experiment was at a very senior manager's meeting. The very senior manager was talking about our bid for Investors in People (A National Standard for Training and Development). I had no idea where she was going with the discussion.

I took a deep breath. Then another.

'Irena. Excuse me for interrupting but I have no idea where you
are going with this.'

The whole room took a sharp intake of breath.

'Neither have I, come to think of it.'

The room laughed, slightly too loudly.

This approach does work, usually. You can get too blasé and lazy. There is a temptation to use this as a 'showing off' tool. On one memorable occasion, I lost concentration midway through a discussion with my boss.

'Well if she's not running the workshop and he's not running it,
then just who is?' I announced smugly.

My manager, never one to let me get away with any nonsense replied, *'You are, you prick. Keep up.'*

It's an excellent tool. Use it wisely. Use it honestly. It could help cut through the corporate code that all large organisations use. And there is a lot of corporate code. Having been on the interviewing end of many promotion boards, I've seen so many reports about saints. Virtually every candidate has never done a bad thing in his or her life, according to their managers. They've never done a bad deed. Never had an evil thought. Then they walk into the room. Please ...

After a while you spend all your time looking through the reports, looking for secret code words. One secret word is 'usually', as in 'Alan is usually calm and even-tempered'. This translates to Alan has psychopathic tendencies. 'Rebecca usually responds well to customers, particularly on the telephone.' This means Rebecca can lose it on the phone now and again.

'Angela is sociable' would be code for Angela can be loud and a party animal and may need to take the odd Monday morning off work with a hangover.

It would be so refreshing to read 'Fred is an ace worker in all aspects apart from figure work. He's useless. He couldn't add up two numbers to save his life.'

I'd promote him. I'd keep him well away from the Accounts Department, but I would promote him.

Recently, I attended a seminar concerning the management of people with mental health difficulties. It was absolutely fascinating. It was on this course, incidentally, that I heard my first amusing mental health joke:

Neurotics build castles in the air; Psychotics live in them; Psychologists collect the rent.

It was full of top tips for managing people who have been off work with mental health problems. One of the best pieces of advice was concerned with how you react to people who are upset. It was a concern for many of us on the course that if we talked to someone who had been away from work for a while they would be prone to getting upset. It wasn't the fact that they'd be upset that bothered many of us – I guess it was the embarrassment we'd feel about it.

'Why?' the course facilitator asked.

'Well – they may get upset and cry.'

'So?'

'Well – it would be embarrassing – for them ... well, I mean for me.'

17

'So, what would you do?'

'Carry plenty of paper tissues with you.' someone remarked.

'Not at all,' the facilitator replied. *'What's the message you're giving out if you pass a tissue to someone who's upset?'*

A silence.

'Aren't you telling them to stop it?' he continued, *'This person feels comfortable enough in your company to show you how they truly feel and you're doing all you can to stop them. Let them cry. What harm is it doing?'*

There were many in the room unconvinced, but it did make me wonder. It took me back to 'telling the truth' – even to yourself. I guess it's the awkwardness it caused me, that has led me to giving people tissues or a handkerchief in the past.

Another great tip that came out of the course for me was to do with preparation for people when they return to work. If you ask them how they are – and you really should – then be prepared for it. Inevitably they will tell you the truth – unashamedly, totally and honestly. That'll be your whole morning gone. You know that, so don't plan anything else.

I heard some similar stories and gained more great tips from an equality of opportunity course I attended a few years ago. It was run by an incredibly successful partnership of disabled people.

The opening exercise was very traumatic for a number of people on the course. The instructors asked us to choose our disability. This was extremely hard. People were getting very upset imagining this. Eventually we'd all chosen – some were blind, deaf, etc.. Then they introduced the second part of the exercise.

'Now, what can't you do?' they asked.

Initially there was a great deal of debate about all the things we couldn't do if we were in a wheelchair, visually impaired or whatever, but after a while and after we had thought about it, there weren't a great many barriers for us. Or at least if there were barriers, there were many ways around them. Most of these obstacles only existed in our heads. Okay, so being blind, I was unlikely to win the 100 metres Olympic title. But as the trainer, very accurately, pointed out, being over forty and not particularly fit would tend to suggest that anyway.

One of the partners who had MS was late coming back from lunch on day one. He arrived in the room thirty minutes late, cursing.

'What happened?' we asked.

'I had to go to the bank,' he said.

'Yes?'

'I asked someone how far it was. She said, "Oh, it's only five minutes down the road." It took me a sodding half hour.'

They had a wealth of stories about how people react to disabilities. My favourite was the other lecturer's story. He said that one summer's day earlier in the year, he was in London, sitting in his wheelchair, outside Marks and Spencer's. He was minding his own business, waiting for his wife and drinking a can of coke.

A middle aged woman walked past, looked at him, opened her purse, took out a pound coin and dropped it in his can. 'There you are dear' she smiled and walked off.

'What do you want us to do?' we asked, *'Ignore you? Help you?'*

'Just tell the truth,' was the answer. *'If you see someone in a wheelchair struggling to open a heavy door say, 'Excuse me – I can see that you're in a wheelchair struggling to open that heavy door – do you need some help?''*

It's not rocket science. It's so simple. So easy. So do it.

<table>
<tr><td>TECHNIQUE
NO 4</td><td>Giving Feedback with Love
and Without Compromise</td></tr>
</table>

'All I want is the truth, Just gimme some truth.'

J Lennon

Let's look at giving feedback. Do we give enough? Do we get enough? I would bet all the money in my pocket that 99% of people would say no to both questions. But what are the reasons behind this. It should be straightforward enough shouldn't it?

Here's an exercise to help look at some of the underlying reasons.

> Take a blank piece of paper. Draw a vertical line straight down the middle. On the left-hand side of the page jot down five separate occasions where you didn't give someone feedback when you should have. This can be anything – from not complaining about a bad meal in a restaurant to not telling your boss what an idiot he was. From not telling a member of staff he has BO to going to meetings you have absolutely no interest in.
>
> Once you've done that look at the first situation and in the right hand column write the reason you didn't say anything. Do this for each situation.

In my experience, working with a variety of managers, the sort of reasons I get in the right hand column are; no time; it's not worth creating a fuss; why bother?; I've tried it before and nothing changed; I don't want to offend.

These are some of the one hundred and one justifications for doing nothing. In essence, for me, this often boils down to some form of arrogance. Let's look at this.

Turn the situation around. If you were on the other end of the situation, would you want to know? If you were the person who had BO, you'd want someone to tell you – wouldn't you? If you owned the restaurant, you'd want to know why you were losing customers – wouldn't you? Of course you would.

So what prevents you telling the other? Underneath it all there may be some sense of your own superiority. Let me explain. Maybe you have the notion, consciously or subconsciously, that they (the recipient) couldn't cope with it. It would upset them. You're basically making an assumption about them that they couldn't handle it. But you could. Therefore you're implicitly declaring yourself better than them. What arrogance! Do you see it? This isn't necessarily done in any nasty, showing off way, but more often than not from a desire to protect the other. It doesn't really matter what your justification is to the other person when they find out … Well – how would you feel?

For instance I heard of someone who was at University doing his final exams. After the last exam, his parents told him his grandmother had died. She had died five days ago and her funeral had already passed. His parents didn't want to upset him at such a vital point in his career. He was distraught and incredibly angry with his parents. He would have liked to have had the choice. You see?

When you're giving feedback, negative or positive, give that feedback on its own. There is a school of thought that says you have to give 'a spoonful of sugar to help the medicine go down'. What nonsense. If you've been asked to see the manager, who rarely sees you except when things are going wrong, you're not going to listen to the first part where she's saying all the nice things. All you'll be doing is waiting for the bad news.

There's the great story of the management consultant who went into a steel factory in South Wales in order to teach people how to give effective feedback.

'It's the bad news sandwich,' he explained. *'Some good news, some bad news, then some good news again. Nice and easy and straightforward.'*

'I'll have a go,' says a steelworker *'I've been waiting for this opportunity to give my manager some feedback.'*

'Okay.'

'Right,' says the steelworker to his manager. *'You're a nice enough bloke, but you're the most useless, ineffective, unreliable, pathetic*

individual I've ever come across in my life.' He walks away, then turns, remembering the theory. *'Oh, and by the way, that tie's pretty nice'.*

Don't give feedback until you can satisfy yourself that you truly understand two important questions.

- Why am I giving this feedback – is it my sole intention to help?
- How am I feeling about giving it?

So why do you give feedback? Do you give it to score points? To show how clever you are? If these are your reasons, then you're wrong and it's not feedback – it's verbal showing off. There is only one reason you should give feedback. You give feedback because you want people to do something differently, to change their behaviour in some way. You should want to help someone. I guess you have no problems in your family or with people you love. *'You're not going out like that are you?'* you'll say.

And be honest with yourself about how you feel. If you feel nervous about it then admit it. If you really wish you didn't have to say it – say that;

'Look Jane, I feel really uncomfortable about this, but I think you need to know that people have started to comment about your personal hygiene.'

Okay, it will help if you can do it skilfully – specific, focused on behaviour, non-judgementally. It will, but that's not the key to this. You can't use the excuse, *'Well I'm no good at this sort of thing,'* as a reason for doing nothing.

You're giving feedback because you love them, or at least respect them enough to want to help them. You want them to do something differently for their sake not just yours, or more specifically you want them to be aware of the impact their behaviour is having on others and give them the opportunity to change it. And you don't need to couch it up in a twenty-minute discussion about all the things they are doing well. Just tell the truth as clearly and as simply as you can. People will forgive you as long as your intentions are to help. Give feedback with love and without compromise.

'I can say, "I am terribly frightened, and fear is terrible and awful, and it makes me uncomfortable, so I won't do that because it's uncomfortable." Or I could say, "Get used to being uncomfortable. It is uncomfortable doing something that's risky." But so what? Do you want to stagnate and just be comfortable?'

Barbara Streisand

So, you've spent six months on a project. You've developed it perfectly. It's neat, clearly labelled, signed off. It looks great on paper. So why isn't anything happening?

Get together half a dozen or so colleagues and run this simple exercise.

Look at your key stakeholders. In terms of this project who are they? Write the name of each one on a post-it. They could be the press, your senior management team, the staff, whoever. Jot all the groups or individuals who have a stake in your project on a separate post-it note. There may well be differences of opinion in your team as to who the key stakeholders are. If that's the case my guess is that everyone's right and include all of them.

Draw the grid overleaf on a flipchart.

Look at each post-it in turn. How would you assess that stakeholder's influence and commitment? For instance, if the HR Department has a high influence in the success of the project, but a low commitment to the project, they would be placed in Section A.

Plot these stakeholders – discuss – disagree – why do you see it differently from others? There will be some valuable lessons here for you. Take some notes.

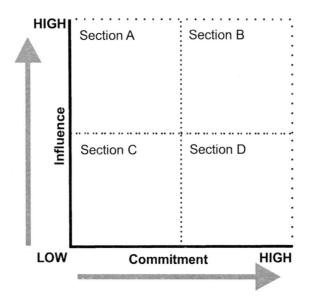

Finally you'll have some sort of agreement. No doubt you'll have stakeholders scattered throughout the grid. Now comes the fun part.

Look at the stakeholders in Sections C and D. Take each post-it off the chart, crumple it into a ball and throw it away. Unless you have unlimited resources – chuck these post-its away – really. And forget about them until the next time you run this exercise. Honestly! You do not have the time or energy to deal with these people. So remove them from your mind.

Next, look at Section B – high in influence and high in commitment – leave them alone. Keep them sweet yes – but again, you can't afford to expend your energy on these people. They are basically okay. They're on your side. Don't upset them!

You've Section A left. These are your targets. Go for them in a big way. Develop strategies to move them into Section B. Look after them. Talk to them – ask them what their concerns are. Address these problems.

This is where the Pareto Principle comes in. This states, among other truths (originally that 80% of wealth is owned by 20% of the population), that the first 20% of effort produces 80% of the results.

For example, I used to work in an organisation that would collect statistics. The accuracy of the statistics was important but equally important was the timimg - there was no point in having accurate statistics published three months too late. The strategy was to phone companies for a particular sector until you had received 80% of the total information you needed. Then people moved on to the next sector. It was found that to collect the last 20% of the informatin took another 80% of the time, so it was better to move on.

When you are addressing the key stakeholders in Section A, keep this in mind. Unless there are absolutely key stakeholders who are capable of stopping the project, target the remainder and use your time effectively. You're not going to be able to spend as much time as you like with all of them so remember the 80 / 20 rule.

Addressing these stakeholders may be uncomfortable. There is probably a good reason why you haven't targeted these people before. We ran this experiment in our training team and identified a group of very senior managers in Section A. We had ignored them and they had ignored us. We were both uncomfortable with each other and 'mutually agreed' to leave each other alone. Although this gave both of us a quiet life, it didn't really help the rest of the organisation . So, we had meetings with them, discussed our concerns and their concerns – both fairly similar in that we both felt slightly intimidated by each other – they perceived us as experts who would be judgmental. We perceived them as people who wouldn't listen to us whatever we said. We started working together with a great deal of success.

This works. It focuses your energies where they are needed. But, things change quickly, so carry out this exercise regularly.

<table>
<tr><td>

TECHNIQUE NO 6

</td><td>

Presentation Skills
and how to 'fake it till you make it'

</td></tr>
</table>

'Oh, you silly old man,
You silly old man,
You're making a fool of yourself,
So get off the stage.'

SP Morrissey

INT – Training Room – North England

'Fake it till you make it.'
Blank looks.
'Pretend you can do something, keep doing it until you wake up one morning and find you really can,.' I continue. *'Pretend you're really confident about presenting. Visualise someone who does it well. Copy them. Really. Trust me – try it – it works.'*
They trust me – they try it – it works – for some of them.

Presentations are the most feared part of most managers' lives. I've read that most managers would prefer the stress caused by moving house than give a ten-minute presentation. To some extent, I get it. It can be intimidating to stand up in front of a roomful of people and talk. In another way, I definitely don't. A lot of the blame must go to 'presentation skills courses'. Yes, it's nice to be able to project your voice to the back of the room. It's great to have exciting slides. It's superb if you can manage the correct eye contact with your audience. Unfortunately (fortunately) within a few minutes of the start of the presentation most of the audience has taken this for granted – however effectively you can carry this out. The message is far more important. Get that right – in your own head – and you're winning.
'What's the worse that can happen?' I ask.
The replies tend to fall into two categories – physical and mental.

29

The physical problems

On the physical side there's the projector failing, nothing to write on, nothing to write with, no chairs, too many chairs, room too hot, room too cold, no one turning up, too many turning up, finishing too early, finishing too late, audience being bored, audience being over excited … Go through these one by one and ask yourself, 'So what?'. Think of everything that can go wrong and plan an alternative. Great. Something you hadn't even thought of will still undo you. Something will not go exactly to plan. You know that. How many things in any other part of your life has gone perfectly? Exactly.

There are some practical things you can do. You must run through your presentation first to get some idea of the timings – ideally you should do this in the room you're going to use, with a few supportive colleagues to act as the audience. Go to the toilet. Take some deep breaths. If you're a woman, wear a long skirt to hide your legs if they start shaking.

The good thing is that people don't judge us on the mistakes we make but on the speed of recovery from those mistakes. Think of the best customer care you've received? Nine out of ten occasions, people recall a situation that went wrong. It went wrong but the service they received to put it right led them to remember it and recommend the company to their friends years later. I've heard stories of a laundry losing most of the clothes but still getting the customer to recommend them. They did everything to make it right. Speed of recovery.

Okay, now that you know there will be mistakes and you've accepted it, truly accepted it – life gets easier. You can arrive early, do all your last minute panicking in peace, relax and wait. People will forgive you if you've prepared as thoroughly as possible. You can't help it if it's the day of a tube strike, the room gets flooded or police have cordoned off the area looking for armed terrorists. It happens.

The mental problems

The second category of things that can go wrong is the mental side – your mental side. You do need to get this right. Preparation is the key, I know it's a cliché but it's also true. This preparation starts right from the moment it's decided you're the one for the presentation. Firstly, do you agree? If not, get out now. It doesn't get easier the longer you ignore it. It's like that sink full of washing up you leave in the kitchen for a few hours, a day, a few days. It never gets easier – just a bit worse, a bit harder to face each day.

Once you've decided it is definitely going to be you – accept it and go for it properly. Do you really want them to know and understand something they didn't know before or do you just want to tell them something and get off? If it's the latter and you just want to impart knowledge, send them an email and save yourself and your audience some grief. If it's the former, then you need to prepare thoroughly. This means that on the day you can throw away your notes, talk and listen. And to listen effectively you've got to involve the audience.

It is so much better for everyone if you interact from the start. Find out what the audience knows and doesn't know. Find out why they're there. Find out their particular interests. Get them involved – they'll enjoy it more and so will you. It may well be more nerve racking than hiding behind a script, but it is so much more rewarding. But this can only happen if you've got your head straight first. To do this you need to ask questions and get them to ask you questions.

How presenters deal with questions by the audience is a tremendous indication of where they are in terms of confidence. If the first line in a presentation is 'I'll take questions at the end' then the odds are that:

a) they are petrified
b) they have no idea what they are talking about, or
c) they have hours worth of material and they'll never reach the end.

You need to take a deep breath, throw away your neat, colour-coded notes and go for it. The audience will certainly enjoy it more and guess what? So will you. I promise.

'Avoid employing unlucky people – throw half the pile of CVs away without looking at them.'

D Brent

Behavioural interviewing is based on the belief that the best predictor of future behaviour is past behaviour. The best way to gauge if a person is going to perform well in a new job is to look at the way they have performed in their current and previous posts. I agree. How could you not? Especially when you look at the alternatives.

'The stress interview sorts the men out from the boys. Put people in a stressful interview and you'll see what they're like in a stressful job'. Oh yes. That'll work, then. Why not pull a gun on them and be done with. There's a story a friend tells of his stress interview with a major bank.

'What if you had to deal with someone who had raped your sister!' screamed the first interviewer.

'But I haven't got a sister.'

'Hypothetically,' came the retort.

'Well, hypothetically, I would put this fact out of my mind. I would treat each occasion as objectively as possible not allowing my feelings to impair my judgement. I would make no assumptions. I would attempt to love and respect this person as an individual. I would try to understand where they were coming from. I would treat each situation on its own merits...'

You get the point. You ask hypothetical questions – you get hypothetical answers. You put people under stress at an interview and they react like they would if they were put under stress at an interview. It doesn't translate to life outside the interview room. Unless the job does involve being shouted at in an interview room – maybe the interviewer was rehearsing a hostage situation? – No it doesn't work does it? If you want to find out how people perform under stress at work, a great line of questioning might be, *'Can you give me an example of a stressful situation you've been involved in at work? Tell me what happened? What did you do?'*

Another alternative is the 'good cop / bad cop' interview – which is truly bizarre. A person you may have known for the past twenty years turns into Torquemada for twenty-five minutes. What does this interview prove? You tell me. I have no idea unless it's a spin on the stress interview. I detest it when interviewers put on their 'I'm a real interviewer' head and refuse to be themselves, laugh or even smile. I know it's a serious business but come on ...

There's the casual interview. *'Hi – just a chat. Let's get a coffee and sit over there,'* pointing at two strategically placed chairs – set at the prescribed ninety degrees to each other – no armrest, low coffee table. There are benefits to this. I like it when that tone is right, both are relaxed and there is genuine information being passed between each other. Unfortunately, most candidates dislike it intensely. It's an interview; it's for a new job, a better job. They want some formality – not a chat with a senior executive in immaculately ironed black jeans.

So what can you do? Well, if you have to conduct an interview (and I'm not convinced this is the best approach in ninety percent of cases) then do it properly.

Tell candidates what's going to happen. Tell them what areas you'll be discussing. Tell them how long they've got. Don't surprise people. If there's a position as a Systems Analyst – ask them questions about that. You wouldn't interview a nanny for your children and ask them questions on thermo-nuclear dynamics would you? Would you? Yet people get asked some odd things? I was asked how I would resolve the miner's strike when I first applied for a computer programmer's job. Other stories abound about 'killer questions' – *'Do fish feel pain?'* was a classic some time ago. *'If a mother and a baby were drowning and you could only save one, which would you choose?'* I was asked a very long time ago. Now I have a little more life experience, my answer would seem to be along the following lines:

'Neither.'
'Neither – then they'd both die?'
'Good.'
'That's stupid!'
'Well you started it.'

Look at the skills required for the job, look at the candidates – match them up. Choose the candidate who's the best fit. The older I get, the easier (some parts of) life gets. I know this is easier said than done. I agree, but it's a lot easier than playing some convoluted game that only interview panel members know the rules to.

It all starts a long time before the interview. Way before the advert goes out. As soon as there's a thought about a job being available, it begins. Define the job. Spell out the skills needed. Advertise these. Send out application forms that are helpful to this process, please. Ask candidates to supply examples they have gathered of them displaying the skills. Don't ask for a set of six skills and send a form out that relates to other skills. *'It's our standard form,'* personnel will say. Argue. Disagree. Refuse. Send out forms related to the job – it will save you so much grief in the long run.

Evaluate the forms matching the evidence (past behaviours) against the job (current criteria). At the interview, you should merely have to fill in the gaps, or build on the examples, or (with any luck) choose between well-qualified candidates. Don't have a list of questions. This can be staid, ridiculous and downright embarrassing. I was once asked if I knew the 'Seven layers of OSI' (it was a buzzword to do with computers at the time).

'I'm sorry, Mr Barry, but I know nothing about OSI.'

He looked at me. He looked back at his notes. *'What's the first layer?'*

'I'm really sorry, Ernie, but I honestly have no idea.'

He didn't even look up 'the second layer' ...

Decide who will ask questions about each of the skills required – teamworking perhaps or management skills. Then explore those areas, look for examples, ask follow-up questions, listen, listen, listen. Don't show off. Let the interviewee guide you. The examples can come from anywhere as long as they meet the requirements. I once interviewed someone for a managerial post – ideally qualified but could supply no evidence of organisational skills.

'Never get the chance to do it in my job – just get given a set of tasks.'

'In your previous job?'

'No, I'm afraid not.'

'Outside work?' I asked desperately.

'Not really,' he said, *'Most of my time is taken up with football.'*

'Oh?' I asked – he looked more like Pavarotti that Pele.

'Yes – I'm secretary of the boys' teams.'

It transpired that he had to deal with twelve teams of various ages, arrange the fixtures, referees, pitches, kits, corner flags ... No organisational skills indeed!

It's as simple as that. Then at the end, watch out for that final question. Candidates can be too relaxed. They've seen the finishing line and anything can happen. Ask something open. Ask if they would like to reconsider some answer they've given, maybe. Ask if they've anything to add. You never know – it could bring results. There was a candidate doing reasonably well until that last question.

'I'm glad you didn't ask me anything about equal opportunities.' He started to dig a hole.

'Why is that?' I asked.

'Well I couldn't never work for a woman again.' He kept digging. *'I worked for one once but, you know, they're different, aren't they. No, never again.'*

'Interesting. Would you like to tell us a little more?'

<table>
<tr><td>

**TECHNIQUE
NO 8**

</td><td>

Leadership I:
Symbolic Acts

</td></tr>
</table>

*'Jesus took bread and blessed it and brake it, and gave it to
the disciples and said, "Take, eat, this is my body." '*
St Matthew Ch 26 v 26

Great leaders have stories, legends, myths about them. These tales
may be totally true, based on some truth or may purely be wishful
thinking, but in some ways it doesn't really matter. They inspire
people. If you're a CEO for a billion-dollar company, you need to be
noticed. You will need to be charismatic (whatever that means) to lead
your staff. Your staff will want stories to tell about you. They don't
want to be led by faceless accountants (no offence, faceless
accountants).

There's the example of a British CEO who took charge of a
confectionery company that was in serious financial difficulty. His first
act was to cut the tails of the sugar mice. What an incredible, symbolic
act. With one gesture he's demonstrating the ruthlessness he's going
to show to turn the company around.

There's the story of Michael Grade, then controller of BBC One – now
Director-General. He was visiting the News Department one day
where they were short staffed. He acted as a junior researcher to
cover a shipwreck story finding a coastguard to interview. People at
the BBC still talk about that today.

Another example is from an internal memo issued in Microsoft,
Germany. Most German industries operated in a very formal manner.
This memo, on the instructions of Bill Gates instructed staff to use the
informal German word for you, 'Du', instead of the more formal 'Sie'.
This very small act was highly significant for motivating the staff and
encouraging them to recognise this new way of working.

It's not all such grand gestures. James Dyson, businessman and inventor, created a superb environment for his staff – subsidised restaurants, no memos, no shirts and ties. The story that sticks in my mind however is what new staff have to do on day one. All new members of staff (whatever grade, whatever salary) have to build a new cleaner themselves and then buy it for £5.

In a similar vein, Edward Guinness (head of Guinness Brewers) recalls his first day in overalls and wellington boots cleaning out huge beer vats.

Names

Perhaps the ultimate symbol for a company is the name. This is the focus – it's what people (hopefully) remember. Would Ben and Jerry's have been as successful if they'd been Cohen and Greenfield's? Would IBM be as world-renowned if they'd stuck with their original title – Computer Tabulating and Recording Company? Would John Wayne have won an Oscar as Marion Morrison? Some brand names seem to have chosen wisely – Maxwell House was, thankfully, named after the hotel the meetings were held at rather than the owner (Joel Cheek). KANGOL (the clothing company with a 4$ billion turnover) was named after the three materials used to make berets in the Second World War (silK, ANGora and woOL). It could have been far worse! It can get even worse. There is the story of the new Italian executive for PowerGen rushing to impress his bosses and securing copyright on the name Powergen Italia!

In crisis ...

On the more serious side, there are a number of acts that organisations make in times of crisis that allow them to stand out from the crowd. In Liverpool, England the Littlewoods Organisation (mail order – largest family owned business in Great Britain, turnover £1.95 billion last year) was founded by Sir John Moores. Each employee who was called up to fight had a personal letter guaranteeing them a job on their return. These letters became legendary. During the Depression, Levi-Strauss CEO Walter Haas kept employees working when there was no meaningful work for them. Malden Mills Chief, Aaron Feuerstein, continued to pay the 2,400 employees after a devastating fire that practically ruined the business. None of these people legally had to do this. It was just 'the right thing to do'.

Women too

There are great stories from history of strong women making grand gestures to inspire and maybe even intimidate men in a world where virtually all the power was in the hands of men. For instance, the naming of the state of Virginia by Elizabeth I sent a powerful message about herself as 'The Virgin Queen' and not prone to the perceived weaknesses of women (at the time) such as bearing children. Another powerful example of a woman asserting herself in a 'man's territory' was Margaret Thatcher's stance against the trade unions forcing the miner's strike in the United Kingdom in 1984. This was a dispute that could have been negotiated yet she chose it as a symbol of where she stood against the power of the Unions.

But it can be the individual

Often in organisations, it's individuals who make the difference. Their values permeate the company and their acts say more than a hundred mission statements ever could. There's another story of Sir John Moores who, as a multi-millionaire, always bought his shoes from his catalogue. On one occasion the supplier knowing who they were for sent a hand-made pair, with fine stitching and soft leather soles. They were immediately returned with a terse note – 'This isn't what I ordered.'

Other individual stories are legendary; When John Harvey Jones took over at ICI he moved all the meetings out of the huge boardrooms and into the smaller offices. Sir Colin Marshall (British Airways) attended every session of his customer care programme 'Putting People First' for staff. Anita Roddick, founder of The Body Shop sponsored posters for Greenpeace in 1985. Lou Gestner (IBM) was reputed to have frequently unplugged the projector during overlong, convoluted presentations by his executives. There was shock in Britain in 1998 when British cookery icon Delia Smith (over

17 million books sold, 25 years as a writer and broadcaster, estimated wealth equal to Princess Diana in 1996) named her 22-part BBC series 'How to boil an egg'. The message was -'I'm going back to basics' and it proved a phenomenal success. Andrew Carnegie's reply on hearing, *'Today, we've broken all records on steel production'* was *'Why not do it every day?'*

These incidents tell us so much about these people and their values, as does one gesture from the world of golf.

It was 1969 and a young Jack Nicklaus in the final match against Tony Jacklin. The team score stood tied. If Jacklin missed, the US team would retain the Cup. Both players were close to the hole and Nicklaus putted first and holed it. Nicklaus picked up not only his own ball but Jacklin's ball mark. He handed it to the Englishman with a handshake, a smile, and an agreed-upon draw. *'I don't think you would have missed that putt,'* said the American. *'But under the circumstances, I would never give you the opportunity.'*

Occasionally the culture of an organisation is so powerful it allows these gestures. For instance, 3M allows scientists 15% of their time to work on their own projects; Benetton's association with expense, glamour and danger naturally leads them to spend $4 million in 1982 sponsoring formula 1 racing team, Tyrell. Herman Miller Corporation formally pegs the CEO salary to 20 times the average earnings in the company.

These stories are inspirational to the people who work in theses organisations. They take business out of the faceless, nine to five, daily grind that it more often than not it. It gives people characters, role models, something to be proud of.

TECHNIQUE NO 9	Leadership II Respect and Never Making People Wrong

'To lead the people, walk behind them.'

Lao-tsu

One aspect of leadership that's frequently ignored is concerned with empathy, respect, care and (dare I say) love that leaders have for their staff. I once worked in a large team for a man we would all do anything for. Why? It was because he always had time for you. He always asked about your family, your football team, whatever was important in your life. We had a number of offices around the country so he often didn't see his staff for weeks on end. However, when he did, he spent the first hour talking to people individually.

Compare that with another way of 'working the room'. A senior manager came along to speak on a training programme. Before he was due to speak we chatted.

'Any of my people here?'

'Two, I think.' I replied

'Oh, who?'

I told him who they were. Blank look. He had no idea who they were.

'Where are they sitting?'

I told him.

He walked in – walked straight over to them. *'Hi, Annie, Hi, Rita. Great to see you again.'*

They beamed. They were absolutely thrilled that a senior manager earning ten times as much as them had remembered their names.

Well, they were until he left and I explained to them how he had manipulated the situation.

There was a survey carried out a few years back asking staff what quality they admired most in their leaders. The result was surprising, well to me at least it was. The top quality was 'honesty'. Interesting, eh?

In an article in *Fast Company*, Tim Sanders, Yahoo Chief Solutions Officer, gives a totally pragmatic reason why you should respect and love your staff, which is concerned with choice.

'At a time when more of us have more options than ever, there's no need to put up with a product or service that doesn't deliver, a company that we don't like, or a boss whom we don't respect.'

So for all the soft options you feel are right and the hard, financial reasons that prove it – it's got to be the right thing to do.

Another facet of this respect for staff is an ability to treat people (all people) especially staff (all staff) with total respect and never making them wrong. I'll explain. Maybe it's easier to illustrate this with a negative situation. I've heard the story of a very, very senior manager in the Civil Service throw his laptop computer at the Head of the multi-million pound Computing Section exclaiming, *'What can I do with this piece of shit. You told me you'd fixed it last week and nothing's changed. Take it away!'* (I've removed the expletives).

I understand his frustration. To many in the office he's a hero – someone who won't take any nonsense from anyone – but I do wonder. Someone once said, *'Don't make someone wrong. If you make someone wrong, they'll get you back.'* Humans, unlike other animals, hate being wrong. It's the second most potent driver.

This was illustrated by the story of an experiment involving rats and humans – made famous by Spencer Johnson in the best seller *'Who Moved My Cheese?'*. A rat is placed in a T-shaped box at the bottom of the T, and some cheese is put in the left-hand corner of the top of the T (got it?). The rat goes to the cheese and eats it. This experiment is repeated a number of times until the rat gets the idea. The next time the experiment is run the cheese is moved to the right-hand corner. The rat goes to the left-hand corner – sees no cheese so goes to the right-hand corner to get the cheese. Sensible. Logical.

Bring in the human. Repeat the experiment until the human gets the idea about where the cheese will be (left-hand corner). Then move the cheese to the right-hand corner. The human goes to the left-hand corner as usual and sees no cheese. He sits down. He waits and waits and waits thinking, *'Someone screwed up – and it's not me.'*

Humans hate being wrong. I'm sure the Head of Computing

Section will get him back – sometime, somewhere. Life has a habit of working out like that don't you think?

The best leaders don't do that. They don't make people wrong. They go out of their way to let people 'lose' with dignity. They manufacture ways out for them – even their opponents. You never know when you might meet them again.

A colleague relates the story of his stressful day going for an interview. He was driving along when someone cut him up. He overtook to see a little old lady totally oblivious to him. Fortunately, he didn't swear at her or send her a rude gesture – he said nothing to her. Of course, you've guessed who was chair of his interview panel.

<table>
<tr><td>

TECHNIQUE NO 10

</td><td>

Motivation
or 'Let's write a real mission
statement, shall we?'

</td></tr>
</table>

*'If you want to build a ship, don't drum up people to collect
wood and don't assign them tasks and work, but rather teach
them to long for the endless immensity of the sea.'*
Antoine de Saint-Exupery

*'How can I motivate the group of disparate, work-shy gits I've
been saddled with?'*
'You can't.'
'Well, this'll be a quick day,' comes the reply.
*'No, really – you cannot get people to do something they don't
want to do – can you?'*
'You can threaten them!'
'Oh that'll motivate them.'
'You can give them more money.'
*'Okay, and that'll work ... for a little while. Within a few weeks,
they're the same as the rest of us – spent it before they've got it. Now
you can really de-motivate them by taking that extra money away
from them. Think about it. You give someone more money for a few
weeks, then put them back on their old rate. Looking at it objectively
they've earned more money than Ms Control working alongside them,
but (and you know where this is going) who's the more motivated
now? Exactly. It's dangerous to play this reward game unless you're
willing to keep upping the stakes, or are prepared to take a great deal
of effort setting it up properly to begin with.'*

A better way for sustainable, non-fragile, 'one thing goes wrong and
we're all fed up again', motivation is to talk about it. Get the team
together and work out exactly why we're here. Write a mission
statement, a set of values, a credo, a code of ethics, a vision, a set of

principles to guide us ... call it whatever you like, but do it and do it properly. Don't get hung up about it being a mission, a vision, a set of principles – just use whatever terms work for you.

Mission statements have a bad press in many organisations. They tend to be decided by a committee of senior managers then handed down to the staff in a similar manner to Moses' set of ten value statements a long time ago. Ask staff what the mission statement is and the reply you tend to get is along the lines of:

'I don't know the words but the tune goes – da da da da da da da da, da da da da de – and there's something in there about being the best, oh ... and teamwork.'

There are some truly great mission, vision statements. The best mission statement with a split infinitive? – *'To boldly go where no man has gone before ...'*. Now that's a mission statement you would come in to work early for, right?

There is the story of a man walking around a large building and asking everyone their vision statement. They could all quote it. They all owned it. They could all see how the effort they put into their job helped to achieve their vision, from the highest paid technicians to the toilet cleaners. The man was John Kennedy and the vision, or challenge was *'To put a man on the moon by the end of the decade.'*

Now, if you can get all your staff to devise and live by your mission statement, your problems are solved. So how do you do it? Well you don't – your people do. It's their statement, their vision and their values – let them come up with it. Give them time, space and the opportunity. Don't give them 20 minutes and then rush them back to work – give them a day, preferably with an overnight stay in a nice hotel thrown in, some decent meals. Let them spend the day identifying the mission, vision and values for the whole organisation.

In terms of the mission statement ask:

● What is the purpose of the organisation?
● What business are we in?'

This isn't always as straightforward as it seems. In the eighties, Parker pens had a crisis. They were losing money as they changed their strategy. They had a high level meeting to try to rectify the situation. The initial thoughts were to cut costs and compete aggressively on price. This was a non-starter. They quickly abandoned this idea. Then they went back to basics and asked themselves what business they were in? If you owned a Parker pen (especially in the sixties) I will bet you received it as a present. The vast majority of people did, still do. So Parker pens decided they weren't in the economy part of the business at all, but in the gift business. This transformed the business strategy. Instead of trying to cut costs they actually made their pens more expensive – better packaging, up-market advertising and it worked. It's still working today.

So back to your organisation – what business are you really in? *'We make pencils.'* Superb start.

Next question. *'Lots of people make pencils. What's so great about your pencils?'*

'Our pencils are better than anyone else's pencils in the UK, no ... in Europe, no ... in the World.' – Okay, now we're getting somewhere. Spend time on this. Find the best ways of describing it. Are they the best pencils in Europe? If not then maybe they should be, or maybe they aren't but they're the cheapest, or the most expensive, or the sexiest, or something.

Once that's agreed, totally and by everyone then you can look at the vision. Think of your organisation in 10 years time. Draw it – if you need to. Yes, get people drawing how they see the future. Not a literal drawing of the finest pencil being produced but try to identify their feelings, their ambition, something real that they can identify

'We want one of our dresses to be worn at the Oscars,' would work. If you can identify something as concrete as this then all you need to do is work out what you need to do to achieve that. Talk about it. Get excited. Set a target, a date, something to aim for. Ask them how will they know when they've achieved it?

'Edward will shut up.'

'Edward?'

'He's our pain-in-the-arse customer who's never satisfied.'

What an incredibly powerful vision –

47

```
┌─────────────────────────────────────────┐
│            To shut Edward up.             │
└─────────────────────────────────────────┘
```

Priceless.

Next you need to work out what business values will help you achieve that. Again, make them real. 'Good teamwork' is nonsense. 'No bitching about people behind their backs' is better. When it happens, you can use these values to address the problems. Get a list – get them agreed – get them used. Best one I've come across recently was 'To what are we committed? Looking good or getting the job done.' If you're committed to getting the job done, you'll make mistakes, you'll try different approaches, you'll ask naive questions – but that's okay – isn't it?

The final part of this is where this process becomes real. Take a break and get your mission, vision and values written up neatly. Then ask the question; 'So, why won't this work.' And list 20 reasons why this won't work. List them all quickly – then go through them slowly and cross them off. Give jobs to people to address problems with real dates (no magic thinking). By the end, you'll have a team that'll kill to achieve their vision – trust me.

Motivation – you needn't worry about it. They'll motivate each other and you as long as they believe.

TECHNIQUE NO 11	**Culture Change Programmes** or 'You'll never get me up in one of those things'

'Nothing's gonna change my world.'

Beatles

'There's a new change management programme starting next week,' said the worried voice on the phone, *'What can I do?'*
'Keep your head down,' was my sage advice.
'But this one's serious.'
'They all are.'
'No – really. This time the HR Department is determined to make it happen. I don't want to change. What can I do?'
'Stay out of the way. It's the Okavanga-Kalahari syndrome.'
'?'
'There's a river in Africa that starts in a range of mountains in Namibia, known as the Okavanga-Kalahari River. Everyone knows where it starts – it's a huge river. It flows into the Kalahari Desert but no one really knows where it finishes. It just sort of fades away.'
'Ah.'

The vast majority of culture change programmes go like this. Big start with trumpets, fanfares, senior managers wheeled out … the first events are hugely popular and over-subscribed. Go back in six months time and ask about it. It just sort of disappeared – no one knew when, or whose decision it was. It just faded into the desert – the Okavanga-Kalahari syndrome.

It's not always so. There are a number of factors that will help in the success of any culture programme.

First – do the maths

How much will it cost? How much extra will you get out of it? If you can't get a tangible benefit, then forget it. Your employees certainly

49

won't be bothered unless there's something in it for them, as individuals. You certainly shouldn't be bothered unless there's something in it for you as an organisation. This benefit should be financial. Okay, it's difficult to measure. Does that mean you don't even try?

'It will make people more motivated and corporate,' is a reason I've frequently heard for running a programme.

'Show me the money,' I reply.

'But we can't express it in financial terms.'

'Try?'

If you can't get a benefit, don't bother. There must be a benefit in terms of more work produced, more targets met, less sick leave taken. Try to calculate all the 'soft' measures. If you can motivate staff to take a real pride in their work, produce quality materials, chase every customer – how much is that worth to you?

Second – attendance on the programme cannot be voluntary

You've done the sums, now make people attend. Make it interesting – that'll help. Make it rewarding. Take people away from the workplace, spend some money on them, treat them decently. They work for you – treat them as you'd like to be treated. Let them travel first class, stay in a nice hotel, feed them good meals with wine. Build this into the maths. Don't be tempted to do it on the cheap.

Third – do the politics

And there will be politics. People tend to not like change, so if you're not getting any resistance – it's because they've heard of the Okavanga-Kalahari syndrome and are just keeping their heads down waiting for it to go away. You need to encourage resistance – get it out in the open. At least here you'll have a chance to address it. If it's hidden in the shadows, you have no chance.

Deal directly with people. Peter Senge describes the *level of alignment* staff have with the vision of the organisation – from committed, working their way down to enrolled, compliant, grudgingly compliant, apathetic or at the bottom, saboteurs. You need to address these saboteurs early on or they will destroy your programme with their cynicism. (By the way, I heard a great definition of a cynic the other day – someone who's given up but not shut up.) But anyway I digress. There are a number of ways of turning 'saboteurs' into stars. One extremely successful method is to get them actively involved in the design of the programme. The most successful 'customer care for computer staff programme' was designed by the three most vociferous opponents of the programme. They were identified very early on and asked to attend the pilot course. They were then invited to help rewrite the programme in the light of their knowledge and experiences.

In one respect, staff can be thought of as sheep. Have you noticed how a flock of sheep move? There are usually a few leaders at the start, a few stragglers at the end and 80% of the flock in the middle. If you can get the first few sheep moving in the right direction along with one or two of the laggards then the flock will head in the right direction. That is as long as you keep them moving. If you stop, there is a tendency for the flock to stop – so build in mini targets, incentives, milestones. Keep the momentum going all the way. Aim for some quick wins to start the sheep moving. These should be tangible, identifiable, public outcomes directly attributable to the programme –

'As a result of the Culture Change Programme there will be:

- *a simplification of the appraisal system*
- *gym membership subsidy introduced*
- *better meals in the staff canteen*
- *a restructure of the senior management team ...'*

A lot of the political difficulties will be caused by the silent majority. Address these. Look at the Shadowside of your organisation. Don't pretend it doesn't happen. There are many examples of this Shadowside at work in organisations. I've been invited to pre-meeting meetings, pre-pre-meeting meetings and even once a pre-pre-pre-meeting meeting to make sure our tactics were correct before the pre-pre-meeting meeting. These activities take time and energy away from the goals of the organisation.

If you ever have to work in a school, on the first day meet the headmaster, of course, and then talk to the people with the real power – the caretakers, deputy headmistresses and their like. In many organisations, Personal Assistants and secretaries tend to have far more actual power than their position in the hierarchy would suggest. Be nice to them. They will get you that five-minute meeting with the Head of Department if they like you.

Don't pretend these things don't go on. Once I worked in an organisation where an administrator who had worked in the office 35 years had a great deal of influence. On the organisation chart, she was very low down, but she had a tremendous amount of influence. If she didn't like something, things tended to move a lot slower, if at all. A new office-wide IT system was introduced. Everything was to be processed using this new system. This administrator had been used to the old system and she took a good few months longer than anyone else to move the training records onto the new system.

Key players

Find out who the key players are, cultivate them. Take up smoking if you need to. The smoking room tends to be a great area for finding out things first. People who go there tend to be relaxed, tend to be from a wide range of work areas and seem to have time to think and make connections. The fact that a computer is being moved and there's been a recent promotion board can give intriguing results – often days before an announcement becomes official.

You must instigate any culture programme from the very top and work down. Managers at all levels must buy into the programme and sell it down the line. This is often a very difficult trick to pull off. Somewhere in the chain there will invariably be managers that 'don't do training'. Talk to them, encourage them, threaten them – whatever works, but you can't ignore them. If staff see managers not attending, or attending and not changing their behaviour, the programme immediately loses credibility. 'Why should I bother?' You'll start seeing lots of non-attendees with 'too busy to attend' notes from their managers. Leading by example has to start from the top and senior managers rewarded or disciplined immediately. If you lose the credibility of the programme, you'd just as well forget it straight away and save yourself some money.

There's a syndrome creeping into modern business now of *change overload*. Every few weeks, there seems to be a new initiative, a new programme, a new mission statement. People are getting drained. Any new programme needs to be real, well thought out, have tangible benefits and fully supported by senior management and all Departments. There should be people begging to go on them. One interesting approach, based on some psychological studies to do with reactants, involved telling people they couldn't attend the programme. They began clamouring to get on it. They were phoning, emailing, *'Why can't I do it? Put me on the reserve list?'* I wouldn't recommend this manipulative use of psychology but there could be some elements of it you could use; invite people to apply, ask them why they should be included, make attendance a reward rather than a punishment. This will work.

Oh, the reference in the title is from an excellent programme concerning change, by Scott Simmerman.

Two caterpillars are talking (as they do) and they spot a butterfly. They both look up and one caterpillar says to the other, 'You'll never get me up in one of those.'

Think about it.

TECHNIQUE NO 12	Managing Change Strategically - in which brainstorming is also explored

'There's none more lost than them that don't know where they're going.'

Bob Paisley

'I phone you up next week. I ask you how do I get to the office, here in Manchester. What do you say?'

'Catch a bus – the number 43 would be best,' someone replies.

'No way – the train's quicker,' another of the group chips in.

'Bus.'

'Train.'

I interject. *'Aren't you missing one key aspect?'*

'You'll never get a taxi,' says a third.

'No,' I patiently reply. *'Isn't there a question you need to ask first?'*

The light dawns for one poor soul. *'Ah, where are you phoning from?'*

'Exactly. I'm actually in Kiev ...'

'So the bus is out of the question, then.'

'Better chance of a taxi though.'

Okay, so it's an unusual scenario but it does highlight one huge problem with managing change. You need to know where you currently are.

In strategic management terms, this is vital but frequently overlooked. Many leaders have a good idea of where they are going – their vision – their goal. However, they seem to have more problems identifying where they actually are at the moment,

There was the classic quote. *'I know exactly where I'm going; it's working out where I am now that's the difficulty.'*

55

Some examples of where it goes wrong

An organisation spends £1.5 million on a new super-duper, all-singing, all-dancing electronic Performance Management System. Dates are agreed, contracts signed and the system is rolled out to the staff on a number of sites throughout the UK. Phase 1 is perfect. Head Office takes a few hours to look at the system, implement it. Then the problems start as reports come back from the other sites. On some sites, the software isn't compatible. On another site, there's a huge number of staff that work in a production area that rarely use computers. Another site has a number of part-time staff that rarely get access to computers and haven't had the necessary training. Oh dear. You get the picture.

The best model to explain this that I've come across is Gerry Egan's Skilled Helper model – known as model B. Like all the best models, it's so simple it feels like cheating. You can use it for strategic management of course, personal development, going to the shops, organisational change, losing weight, anything. It was originally developed as a model for helping with the counselling process and is widely used in counselling skills.

In strategic management terms it works best as a totally pragmatic, straightforward set of questions you need to answer to enable you to move in.

Very basically, it's:

- Step 1 – where are you now?
- Step 2 – where do you want to get to?
- Step 3 – how will you get there?

- Step 1 – I'm in Kiev.
- Step 2 – I want to get to Manchester.
- Step 3 – Let's look at different options to get there.

Okay, so your problem may be a little more complicated than that but the principle's the same. The model breaks each stage down into a number of steps

Step 1 still looks at the current situation but breaks it down into three parts:

a. What's the story? What's going on? What is the problem?

b. What's really the problem? What is it that the organisation charts aren't showing? (This is an aspect that's often overlooked. You need to take a great deal of time and effort to find out what's happening. This would have helped uncover the lack of computer skills on a number of sites).

c. What is important here? Of all the things you uncover in a and b, which are the key ones that will help the most? Which are the key dominoes that you could push that will get the other ones to move?

Don't be tempted to rush through this part of the process. I guarantee this will save you a great deal of time, money and upset in the long term. Trust me.

Let's give you a scenario. I've been left something from my eccentric grandmother – it's four factories full of paper clips (I told you she was eccentric, didn't I?). Each factory hold roughly 5,000,000 paper clips – that's the good news.

Part b of this little scenario is that there is no market for paper clips – there has been a recent invention that has superseded paper clips. So we have set the scene. Now, what's important? To me, it's money. I want to get as much money as I can as quickly as possible.

Now comes the fun part. What are some of the options available? This is where a group of people really helps. Let's brainstorm how I can change these assets (warehouses, paper clips) into money. Over the past few years, I've run this exercise a number of times and constantly been amazed by the number of ideas it has generated. Brainstorming must be set up properly with a few clear rules – no judging, no questioning, ideas as ridiculous as possible, anything goes – lots of energy …

The best story I've heard of a brainstorming sequence relates to telephone wires in Canada. These wires were covered with snow for long periods, which became heavy and resulted in many broken wires. There was a brainstorming session arranged to generate ideas on how to resolve this problem. The session went something like this.

'How will we get snow off the wires?'
'Get the polar bears to shake the posts.'
'How will we get the polar bears to shake the posts?'
'Put meat on the top of the posts.'
'How will we get the meat up on the posts?'
'Get helicopters to drop the meat.'
'But when the helicopters fly over the wires ...'
'They'll dislodge the snow!'

And apparently that's what they did. They arranged for helicopters to fly above the wires dislodging the snow.

Back to my paper clips. Some of the best ideas generated have been what to do with these obsolete paper clips – jewellery, scrap metal, body armour have just been a few of the ideas. My favourite was 'coat hangers for action men'.

Once you've exhausted the ideas, get the group to vote for their favourite and then look at the final option – getting there. How will you turn your idea into reality? Get real – no magic thinking – send people away to do the research and come back with a solid plan of who's doing what and when.

This generally works really well. People seem to buy into the process. The real beauty of this is that you can use it for practically anything. It was devised for counselling and is used extensively throughout many counselling fields – divorce, bereavement, child psychology, etc.. but you can use it for personal development, managing your time, and even working out the best journeys.

TECHNIQUE NO 13	Listening or there's more to communication than just talking

'The reason why we have two ears and only one mouth is that we may listen the more and talk the less.'

Zeno of Citium

People are odd. People are difficult. People have their own ideas, thoughts and agendas. People are pretty much as mixed up, confused and vulnerable as we are. People are basically pretty much like us.

As a manager you get to manage people. People have problems. You have problems and you as a manager have to manage people's problems. It's not a surprise. It goes with the territory. You can't really complain, can you? It's like doctors complaining that they only ever get to work with sick people. It's what happens.

There are ways of helping. These ways all involve just a few basic skills but a great deal of time. You need to give people a great deal of your time in order to help them. This can be a pain. Your member of staff with a problem won't turn up to see you on a boring Wednesday afternoon when you've planned two hours of 'helping' time, booked a room and got yourself psyched up for it. Oh no, they'll turn up 4 o'clock on a Friday afternoon when it's frantic, there's a 5 o'clock deadline, it's raining and the only available free space for a quiet word is the car park.

To help people you need to use the 3-L skills – listen, listen and listen. Find somewhere quiet, let them know how long you've got and listen. Let them talk. Don't advise them, don't hurry them up, and don't blame them. Just listen.

Don't advise them means just that. If you give them advice, you can't win. If it's the best advice in the world – they'll be back next time for more advice and more time. If it's wrong – they'll be back to blame you. You can't win by giving advice.

Let them talk. Let them find the answers to their problems. There

59

are a number of ways you can get this totally, horribly wrong.

Wrong approach number one – she tells you her problem in
agonising detail. She hasn't slept in weeks. She's distraught.
   Your reply, '*Well, serves you right. You shouldn't have got
involved with him in the first place. What did I tell you at the
time? I told you he was a bad one ...*'

Wrong way number two. Similar scene – distraught member of staff,
painstaking detail about his financial problems – children not
eating, bank threatening to take their house away from them.
   Your measured and skilled response, '*You think you've got
problems. You should have a look at my bank statements some
month – I've barely enough to keep the child in public school, and
the cost of her violin lessons. Have you any idea how much it costs
to keep a pony these days?*'

Stop. Do you think they want to hear this? It's reminiscent of the time
I played golf with someone I'd never met before. By the time we'd
reached the half way stage, I was ready to walk off the course.
Everything I'd done, he'd done bigger, better, quicker, easier ... I told
him that I'd just come back from a week in Scotland – he'd been for
two weeks. I told him I'd played Saint Andrew's new course – he'd
played the old course. I'd lost four golf balls; he'd lost ten. I'm sure
if I told him I had an elephant in the garden he'd have had a bigger
elephant.
   Don't fall into this trap. You're not helping anyone. Listen, listen
and listen. By listening, I don't mean you have to sit in total silence
staring out of the window. Listen actively. Show that you're listening
with those 'ohs' and 'ahs', little grunts and groans, nods and smiles
that we all make when really listening. But really listen when you do
them. It's no good smiling encouragingly as they tell you how upset
they are because their parrot had to be put down. Use these
paralinguistic skills appropriately. Ask questions to clarify. You can
give factual advice but make it non-judgmental and as neutral as
possible. No '*If I were you ...*' statements please.

Some techniques to help this listening process come from the types of statements you make as a listener. These techniques involve paraphrasing, reflecting and summarising. This gives your listener time to consider, and ensures you're on the right track.

A response from you could be, *'So, if I've got this right, you think your options are:*

1 *take the job in South-east Azerbaijan*
2 *leave the kids with your mother in law and lock yourself in the garden shed for a week, or*
3 *go home and have a good lie down.'*

Do this non-judgementally, but caringly. With practice, you'll be able to pick up what people aren't saying through their body language, tone of voice, and what they're actively avoiding.

(An aside on body language. There are a number of books on this. All of them describing gestures, movement, sitting, standing. Absolutely fascinating – if that's what you like. My short paragraph summary for body language follows.

If it doesn't feel right, it probably isn't – so check it out. If the person you're talking to's body language doesn't quite 'match' the words, tell them, *'Look, I might have got this totally wrong but when you're talking about being an open, caring, sensitive soul and you're playing with your dagger, it doesn't quite fit for me.'* It may be more subtle than that but the same principle applies. *'When you're talking about feeling fit to come back to work, there's something in your body language that doesn't quite match it. Are you sure you're ready?'*)

These skills will take time and can be frustrating as you know (or think you know) the answer. Wait for them to get there. Give them the space and trust that they will get there. Oh, and don't expect thanks. They'll be convinced they did everything themselves. So this is a very 'adult' process for you to go through.

There will be times when these rules don't apply. Times when common sense will prevail. If someone comes rushing up to you asking for the toilet, don't smile encouragingly and ask them to elaborate on their feelings. Tell them.

There may be occasions when you need to use some techniques to get people to open up or to help them think things through. Keep these techniques in your back pocket and use them when you need to. Don't let these techniques get in the way of your listening.

A very useful technique for getting people to focus on resolving problems comes from a counselling book, *The Skilled Helper* by Gerry Egan. I love it because it's so simple. So simple yet so powerful. There are only three basic stages in helping.

Stage 1 – find out where they are.
Stage 2 – find out where they want to be.
Stage 3 – get them to work out how they get from where they are to where they want to be. Familiar?

- Where are you now?
- Where do you want to be?
- How can you get there?

It's used extensively in counselling. An example could be in divorce counselling.

Where are you now? This would lead to lots of lively debate about the current situation, who's fault it is and so on. Counsellors are trained to listen carefully, non-judgementally and keep the discussions focused. Eventually you'd find out where people are and how they felt about the situation.

The skilled counsellor would now be able to move on to the second stage – so, *where would you want to be?* This would eventually, hopefully, lead to some common understanding and agreed aims. Once this is clearly established the third stage of getting there would need to be sorted out.

If you've got this framework clear, you can help people work through it. You may not need to say anything, or you may need to ask questions to get them to find out where they are, what they want and how they'll get it. Again, the key to this is listening.

Okay. It sounds straightforward, but you know it's not. People are funny. People are odd. People tend not to talk, especially when upset, in clear distinct stages. Problems tend not to stand alone but be part of other problems. Life gets in the way. Helping someone to solve a problem may take days, weeks, months or even years. You know you've got to though, don't you. The alternatives are far worse.

Another very helpful book is *Counselling Fundamentals in the Workplace* by David McNorton, published by Management Books 2000.

> *'All animals are equal but some animals*
> *are more equal than others.'*
>
> G Orwell

In times of organisational change, it is estimated that 80% of a manager's time is spent dealing with non-strategic 'stuff'. This 'stuff' is what Gerry Egan calls 'The Shadowside of Organisations'. Gerry Johnson and Kevan Scholes call it 'The Cultural Web', but it's basically the same 'stuff'. It's the culture of an organisation.

Even in times of relative calm, a great amount of a manager's time is spent dealing with the dark side of the organisation. This comprises everything that is not written down. You won't find it on an organisation chart, or a business plan. It's 'how we do things around here'. It's the glue that holds an organisation together. It's not always negative though. For instance, if you have an organisation 'working to rule' as frequently happened in the 1980s, logically, you could think it would make no difference. We know differently. It's those little things people do for each other that make things work – that teacher covering another class, the manager helping out on the shop floor, the sudden request for overtime met.

However, a great deal of the shadowside can be negative and time consuming. These models (the Shadowside and Cultural Web) force managers to look at their organisations, find the shadowside practices and deal with them. For instance those pointless weekly meetings – when challenged about why they are held, I have frequently been told 'because we've always had them.'

Frequently these practices say more about the organisation than any mission statement does. A major retail organisation I once worked for had a very clear, but unwritten, attitude to managers and money. One manager was taking money to the bank at lunchtime and was attacked by youths with baseball bats and the money was taken from him. After he left the hospital, he was at the police station for a long time. The organisation's first thought was always that the managers are involved unless they can prove otherwise. This was told to me on my first day.

One dry cleaning company a colleague recently visited would like to pride itself on its delegation of authority to shop managers. The colleague wanted to have a jacket dry cleaned. The cost was £10. She then spotted that week's offer – any two items cleaned for £8.

'Does this include jackets?' she asked.

'Yes,' replied the manager.

'So, can I have the jacket cleaned for £8 then?'

'No. It says any two items and you've only got one.'

Amazed, my colleague took a sock from her two-year old baby and handed that and the jacket to the manager.

'That'll be £8 please.'

Compare that with Ritz-Carlton who have a policy to never lose a customer. Whoever receives a complaint has to own it, resolve it to the guest's satisfaction and record it. All their staff are allowed to spend up to $2,000 without referring to their supervisors to resolve customer problems on the spot.

In a similar vein, Stew Leonard staff are empowered to reject anything that isn't perfect. If the employee unloading a delivery doesn't like the look of the strawberries they can reject them without referring to anyone else. They have a sign – 'If it's not good enough for your grandmother, don't put it out for the customer'.

There are a great many organisations out there that have written values about equality – 'all our staff are equal', 'everyone's a person in this workplace'. Yet how often have I seen different rules for different people. Senior managers get to travel first class, executives get to stay at more expensive hotels, car parking spaces are reserved. These shadowside models give people the right to challenge these practices. I'm not advocating the abolition of differences (well, I am really, but that's another story), but rather the honesty of the espoused values. If you're not going to treat people equally, don't say you are. Once these inconsistencies have been identified, you can make a great change to the culture. Get rid of reserved parking spaces for senior managers, allow everyone to travel first class. These symbolic gestures will make a big difference..

The culture of an organisation can have a big impact on all aspects of the business. Many organisations say they have an open culture but how many have the culture of an organisation like Hewlett-Packard? Here they really do have an 'open corporate culture'. At the end of the day, projects are not locked away in desks but left out for others to look at, pick up and work on. This ego-free attitude seems to work as they have a $72 billion turnover and need to be innovative – 60% of their sales are from products developed within the last two years.

It's not always the organisation chart that shows where the power lies in an organisation. Many years ago, I was training to be a teacher. One of the lecturers was incredibly astute. Unusually for our lecturers he had real experience of teaching in secondary schools. He has spent the majority of his career as a teacher, then a headmaster in a variety of schools. The last lecture from him before we went out on teaching practice for the first time went as follows.

'Who is the most important person in the school you're going to work at?' he asked.

'The headmaster or headmistress,' we sang in unison.

'Not usually,' he replied. *'Listen carefully.'*

We leaned forward.

'The key people in schools tend to be the caretakers. They have a lot of control, a lot of power. If the caretaker doesn't want it to happen, it rarely happens. Secretaries are also important, as are Deputy Headteachers. Keep on the good side of all these.'

This principle holds true for most organisations. On another level altogether, I can only quote verbatim from Nelson Mandela's autobiography dealing with his time in prison on Robben Island.

'The most important person in any prisoner's life is not the minister of justice, not the commissioner of prisons, not even the head of prison, but the warder in one's section. If you are cold and want an extra blanket, you might petition the minister of justice, but you will get no response. If you go to the commissioner of prisons, he will say, "Sorry, it is against regulations." The head of prison will say, "If I

*give you an extra blanket, I must give one to everyone." But if you
approach the warder in your corridor, and you are on good terms with
him, he will simply go to the stockroom and fetch a blanket.'*

It's a similar, if less dramatic, story in most organisations. Personal
Assistants are a very powerful band of people. They can get you that
ten-minute interview with the boss, or they can stop you seeing her
for weeks. Be aware of the important people in your organisation.
Smoking rooms used to be essential places for finding information in
large organisations. You'd often get a wide range of people, at all
grades who knew little bits of the jigsaw; someone would know of a
new post, someone else would have to set up a new pc, and suddenly
pieces fit. I'm not advocating being a gossip and pretending to smoke
to find out what's happening. I am saying be aware of what's going
on around you.

'Yes, but Marge, you're missing the point! The individual doesn't matter. It was a team effort, and I was the one who came up with the whole team idea ... me!'

H Simpson

There are a mass of excellent (and expensive) guides and profiles to analysing and perfecting teams – there's TMS, Belbin, Myers-Briggs, ETMP, personal drivers ... just to name a few. So how come they don't all work perfectly. In your teams, you can get the perfect mix of extroverts/introverts, concluder-producers/creator-innovators, team workers/resource investigators, Virgos/Scorpios – but still your team doesn't turn out right. Why is that?

The best illustration of this comes from an intensive management development programme I ran a few years ago. All week we'd been looking at a variety of ways to build a team and had everyone profiled; Bill – introvert, analytical, plant, Scorpio rising, creative, hurry-up driver, favourite Beatle – Ringo; Jane – implementer, extrovert, Aquarius moon, be perfect driver, if I could identify with an animal it would be a leopard; and so on. Then the final exercise involved splitting into two teams and competing against each other in a management case study exercise. Three members defined as analysts had a field day – they matched and matched – a creative-introvert for each team, a co-ordinator in each group, and so on and so on. Finally the teams were announced. *'Any problems?'* one of them announced smugly. A shy voice spoke out. *'Uh, yes,'* she said. *'I want to be in the same team as my friend.'* So the teams were restructured – boys versus girls – and a great success.

This is not to decry these team building tools – but remember they are just that – tools to use wisely and appropriately. I've found that they're not that good for initially choosing teams. The key factors they don't (can't) quantify is that 'humanness' that we all have. That chemistry that happens or doesn't happen between people. They are good for a number of other reasons though – they're good for getting some idea whether the person will be good in the role, and they're great for developing the team and the individual later in the team's development.

Have a look at the job – if it involves public speaking, persuading people, motivating the rest of the team – I guess you're looking more at the extrovert side of the scale – usually. Unless you're paying an awful lot of money, or someone really, really wants to develop these skills, I'd avoid the introverts.

Once the team starts working together, these profiles can really come into their own, but we'll come back to that. Use the traits to get people talking about what they prefer, what role they would like. These profiles are superb for giving people the excuse to be proactive. The creators see that they've an opportunity to work as creators so will fight for it. The analysts finally get a chance to do what they would like so they become more expressive. It works really well.

Stages of group development

Alongside this, the work of Bruce Tuckmann starts to kick in. His model of the various stages effective teams go through is excellent. Over time, teams move from forming to storming to norming to performing. **Forming** is the polite stage teams go through when they're getting to know each other – the very polite, 'more tea, vicar?', 'after you', 'no, after you' stage. The next stage is the **storming** where the team are more confident and there are disputes over status, roles, etc. This needn't be loud and violent, it could be dark and quiet, or sarcastic, but it needs to happen for the team to evolve. The team have to be able to bounce ideas off each other and disagree with each other. In the **norming** stage the team have worked out their roles and can relax ready for the **performing** stage where there's a real buzz.

You know this is true, don't you. If you walk into a room to meet your new team and there's deathly silence – be afraid, be very afraid. Team rooms should sound like infant school classrooms – lively and buzzing yet focused. If you've worked in a team for three months and someone still needs to ask if they can borrow a pen from the pile on your desk, you're in trouble. There should be discussion, disagreements, people should feel some passion about their work. Think Oasis – the best pop band of the nineties who were forever 'storming'.

So, how do you deal with (encourage even) the storming? This is where the profiles can come in handy. They almost give the team a license to storm. During team building sessions, you hear things like,- *'Well when that happens it really winds me up – that's Upholder Maintainers for you'*. It becomes more impersonal. People really do open up even though they hide behind the labels. Now you can do something about it.

In terms of the Team Management System devised by Margerison and McCann, I'm a Reporter Advisor – flexible, beliefs-driven, introvert and creative. My co-trainer eight years ago was exactly the opposite – structured, analytical, extrovert and practical. We'd be running a five day course and really start annoying each other. I knew that on day two at 11:18 if it were his session, we'd be looking at stage two of Maslow's hierarchy of needs. 'Get a life' I'd urge (silently) – he was a lot bigger than me. He knew that sometime on day three or four we'd get around to Adair's action centred leadership model. 'I wish he'd get his act together,' Desmond would think (not also silently) – has was aware of how sensitively I used to take criticism in those days. Then we were profiled and talked about this. Now we know why we get on each others' nerves occasionally and have a far greater understanding of each other – we recognise we are different and see the world differently.

This will work for your team. What may not work, unless you handle it extremely well is a 'fun team-building day'. Never tell your team they're going to have fun – I can hear people groaning already. They would rather spend a day in a corner doing hard sums that be dragged along to a fun awayday. Make it work related. They'll create the fun themselves. Make all activities relate to some aspect of work – people really would prefer it.

If you've just inherited a team, this day is essential. It'll give you a great insight into the people you've got. There are some very, very simple exercises to help this.

Exercise one – get the team to draw how they see themselves. If they draw themselves as slaves on a galley ship with their previous manger and senior managers as the drum beater, whip handler and captain, run away. If they draw themselves as flowers and the previous manager as the sun, run away quicker. I'm joking – but you get the point.

Another superb exercise is to get them to agree on the top teams from anywhere. I've seen the top teams named as ants, Ferrari formula one team, 1966 England world cup football squad, Microsoft, various British Lions rugby teams, surgeons, Amazon.Com. Then look at what makes them so special and emulate that – ants were felt to be totally supportive to all other members of the team, non-blameful (although no one checked) and very focused. That worked. It was fun.

TECHNIQUE NO 16	Choice

'What are you rebelling against, Johnny?'
'Whaddaya got?'

M Brando

There are two classic studies of choice/lack of choice that could be incredibly powerful for managers. There is the work carried out by Ellen Langer on the perceptions people have on choice and Jack Brehm on restriction of choice and the impact that has. Both are fascinating, both could be incredibly useful.

The experiment by Ellen Langer in 1975 consisted of selling $1 lottery tickets. One half of the experiment group received a randomly selected ticket; the other half got to select their own ticket.

Then she tried to buy back the tickets. The group that had received a randomly selected ticket took on average $1.96. The second group (who had control and a choice) wanted an average of $8.67. The tickets had the same chance of winning, obviously, so why the difference? I would guess that it's the perception of choice that is important here. If you are in control and take ownership, you are more likely to value it. I would guess this is the reason most people don't wash a hired car – it's not theirs.

Linked to this is the concept of reactants explored by Jack Brehm. Be aware of reactants when dealing with people. 'Reactance occurs when someone perceives his or her freedom being denied or limited.'

In other words, if you tell someone they can't doing something there will be a tendency for them to do it even more. You know that though, don't you. If you've got children, you've got empirical evidence.

My colleague recounts the story of his 16-year old son who had argued all evening as he was getting ready to go out. Finally he's ready and my colleague shouts,

'Have a good evening!'

'Stop telling me what to do.' comes the reply.

Brehm would say that this is inbuilt to some degree and we can use it, as managers, for good or evil. This can be used manipulatively in sales, especially. It's known as 'The take away technique'.

You are listening to the sales person and things are going okay. She's shown you a number of kitchens you could be interested in but aren't sure. Then she says that you can't have one of them. Up to this point you haven't been particularly bothered as to which kitchen, car, mobile phone you would choose. Suddenly you are.

'Why can't I have this one?'

'Oh, you couldn't afford it – it's a bit more expensive than the others ...'

Like a fish on the end of a line – you've been hooked and before long you're begging her to let you buy it. This isn't big and it isn't clever – it's manipulative and you'll never trust that salesperson (or any other) for a long time after you realise what's happened.

But reactance can be useful. It's powerful and, as a manager, you should be aware of the power of denying or allowing control. You should allow as many genuine options as possible to your staff. This may not necessarily be in terms of the outputs, but in terms of the process for achieves those outputs. If you can, define the output – quality, quantity, time, cost and let the staff work out the best way of achieving it.

There is also a link to stress in this. Apart from the stress caused by too much work, a great deal of stress is caused by little, or no control. Give staff more control and you'll have less stress, happier staff and a more motivated workforce.

The ultimate example of allowing workers freedom comes from Ricardo Semler. In his organisation, Semco, workers have a great deal of freedom. They have the freedom to choose their boss, their salary, their working hours. Each employee receives the company's financial statements and attend classes on how to interpret them. Semco has no receptionists, secretaries or personal assistants. And it really does work. It's a truly democratic organisation.

Researchers Robert Tannenbaum and Warren H Schmidt looked at the process of choice and delegation. Their result was the Tannenbaum-Schmidt continuum. It shows seven degrees of managerial control and staff freedom.

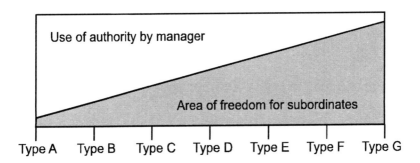

Type A	-	Manager makes decision and announces it.
Type B	-	Manager 'sells' decision.
Type C	-	Manager presents ideas and invites questions.
Type D	-	Manager presents tentative decision subject to change.
Type E	-	Manager presents problem, gets suggestions, makes decision.
Type F	-	Manager defines limits; asks group to make decision.
Type G	-	Manager permits staff to function within limits defined by superior.

Tannenbaum and Schmidt Continuum

They range from the extremely autocratic type A management style 'Just do it' to type G 'You tell me how you're going to do it.'

There are advantages and disadvantages of each managerial position and each situation would need to be treated on its own merit but there are a number of common themes that emerge.

Let's run through a few examples. Suppose the manager had a new team of staff just started and it was their first day in the office and there was a fire alarm. In terms of the continuum, where would be the most effective style for the manager to adopt? I guess we'd all agree somewhere close to type A would work. I wouldn't be in favour of a group discussion with staff discussing the merits/demerits of any particular escape plan. Let's be direct – *'Go through that door, down the stairs and out,'* would work for me.

On the other hand if the manager wanted to increase sales on a particular product that all his sales staff were familiar with, it would be a good option, I think, to allow them as much scope as possible. After all, they are the ones that will need to sell it. Let them choose the method. The more freedom they have, the more ownership they'll feel and the more motivated to make it work.

The learning here for the manager is to leave people alone as much as possible. It may be difficult – especially when you know (or at least think you know) the answer. Let people work it out for themselves.

If it's time critical (as with the fire) or it's already been decided by you, or head office, or its the law, then don't waste time holding meetings pretending staff have an say in whether it's implemented or not, but if there is any opportunity for freedom let people have that freedom.

This needs a very mature manager. You have to trust your staff. It's still your fault if things go wrong. It's delegation, not abdication, and you have to let the staff take the credit when things go well. But they will perform well, more often than not. People want to do a good job. People, in my view, don't come to work to waste time, be unpleasant or cause trouble – people come to work to be creative, do a good job – they just want the opportunity to do that. Why not give them that opportunity? It's your choice.

<table>
<tr><td>

**TECHNIQUE
NO 17**

</td><td>

Staying in the Wanted and Needed Conversation

</td></tr>
</table>

*'Your debutante knows what you need –
but I know what you want.'*

B Dylan

'Yes, of course I'll do that for you,' you'll say, then spend the next three weeks worrying about what you've agreed to, how you'll find the time to do it and ultimately how can you get out of it.

When you negotiate, discuss or whether you just plain agree to do something, you need to go through a strict process. It may seem hard and time consuming but trust me, when you get into the habit, it'll save you so much time and anxiety that you'll wonder how you survived before.

A great amount of time and effort is expended because people haven't had a meaningful discussion. In terms of Boroto/Zahn – 'an effective wanted/needed conversation'. This is the key to any form of negotiation. Both parties need to establish exactly what's required, by when, by whom and where the responsibilities lie.

The truly gifted negotiators have learnt to handle this part of the conversation extremely effectively. They communicate skilfully by talking and listening and 'staying in the conversation' until they are totally sure of the goal. Staying in the conversation can be difficult. How often have you been introduced to someone and not caught their name? Do you ask them to repeat it? How often? A skilled communicator should ask for as long as it takes – we all know the problems if we don't do this. We spend the rest of the evening avoiding the person, or feeling embarrassed when we talk to him. This can go on for weeks. I've known people that didn't catch someone's name the first day at the office and as the weeks have gone by, become too embarrassed to ever ask them.

So, back to the *wanted and needed conversation* – you need to establish what the other person truly needs, not just wants. For instaffnce, in my role as a consultant, I frequently met managers who wanted 'a team building day'.

'That's what I want and that's what I need,' they would claim.

There needed to be a great deal of skilful communication to tease this out, starting with lots of open questions along the following lines.

'Why do you feel you need this?'
'What are the problems now?'
'What do you want this team-building day to achieve?'
'How will you know if this event is successful?'
'How will be able to demonstrate this?'

Ask questions and listen to the replies. Invariably what the person needs doesn't match with what they think they want initially. Team-building days tend to occur when there are a few members of staff disrupting the team, or the team aren't clear about their roles, or there's no direction from the leader, etc. You need to listen, investigate and probe until you find out what the real problem is. Then be as specific as possible about this problem and ensure the other is absolutely clear about it and what she now wants and needs. Only now, when you've got something tangible to work with can you begin to start looking at solutions.

The key to this is asking effective questions. And how do you ask effective question, you ask? You ask effective questions when you listen skilfully. You listen to the person, what he says, what he doesn't say, how he says it. Listen to that little voice inside you. If something doesn't feel right, it usually isn't. Do it now rather than in a few weeks time when you're working with a hundred staff. If you aren't sure then, ask. This needn't be a big thing. Just tell the truth.

'Well, you say there's no problems between any of the staff, but I have a feeling there may be. Can you tell me a bit more about this?' Stay in that conversation until you have no doubts at all and are completely sure of what's expected. This may seem incredibly strange to begin with but, trust me, it will save you so much stress in the long term.

The next part of the discussion is about your willingness and ability to meet that request – a 'Willing and Able Conversation.' You need to honestly ask yourself whether you are willing and able to meet the request. Have you the necessary skills, knowledge, attributes to make it work. If you haven't, then say so and try to work out a way to still help – suggest others, look at different approaches, but again 'stay in the conversation'. If you are willing and able to help, then great. Even then, don't stop and walk away before you're absolutely 100% sure you know what's expected of you. You know from experience that if you're not sure, that this won't work, don't you? The 'problem-solving fairy' doesn't miraculously appear and sort things out when you ignore them. Problems don't just stay quiet and disappear. They just stay there and grow and grow. It's a bit like the washing up you meant to do yesterday, or the day before – it won't sort itself out. It'll just get a little harder to deal with each day.

So, deal with these problems as they arise. Stay there until you're happy, the other is happy. This all seems so clear and sensible I know, but it can be difficult. The good thing though is that it does get easier. The more you do it – the easier it gets.

'In truth, a good case could be made that if your knowledge is meagre and unsatisfactory, the last thing in the world you should do is make measurements. The chance is negligible that you will measure the right things accidentally.'

G Miller

Go along to any medium/large organisation and offer to save them £1,000,000.

Ask them to give you three good reasons why they should keep their Performance Management System. If they can, ask them to put a cost of these benefits. Call this figure 'A'.

Then ask them to calculate how much time, money and effort goes into the upkeep of this system. Cost the number of hours it takes all staff, management, personnel, other administrators and programmers to maintain this system. Call this figure 'B'.

Now do the maths. If A > B keep the system. If A is not > B then stop running the system. The difference between B and A can run into millions of pounds.

Is it this simple? Maybe not, but it's a great place to start.

In general, Performance Management Systems, Appraisal Systems, whatever you'd like to call your system, are, at best, not used as effectively as they could be in organisations. At worst, they are demotivating, divisive and worse than having nothing at all. They are too often seen as a hindrance to managers. They get in the way of 'real work'. They are brought out of the bottom drawer once a year, briefly discussed with the best of intentions then put back in the drawer for another year.

It seems to be a symptom of an organisation that the more unhappy the staff are, the more structured and rigorous the Performance Management System is. You've worked for/with people you've liked, trusted and respected, haven't you? I guess you didn't need a piece of paper at the end of the year to tell you how well you or they were doing in a range of competences.

If it were your own business, would you give yourself a Performance Agreement? I don't think so. Why wouldn't you? Because you know what you've got to do and you don't need it written on a piece of paper. Similarly, if you employ a handful of staff – everyone knows what's expected of them because you talk about it, learn from each other and apply your collective knowledge. So why impose this on others. For the vast majority of systems, there is little commitment for the system throughout the organisation. It's a chore. There is more time spent chasing people to follow the correct procedures than there is analysing the results.

These systems do work, but only where there is a genuine commitment from all levels to use them effectively. This is not impossible.

- You need to set your objectives with all stakeholders involved.
- Determine what really is expected of people – everyone to perform effectively. This must be measurable.
- Spend as much time as you can to determine the standards expected.
- Try to develop a culture of looking at outputs rather than processes.
- Give people the autonomy to meet their targets in their own way.

For salespeople, this last one seems to work really well. If a salesperson has a target of selling 500 things a month within a budget of £1,000 and they meet it – brilliant. As long as they do nothing illegal or upset everyone on the team, and behave ethically, that's really good news. As their manager, I wouldn't be concerned if they sold 500 things on day one and had the rest of the month off, because they were superb sellers. Or, if it took them until 11:59 on the last day of the month because they were awful (there may be other issues involved here but you get the idea?).

Outside the sales environment it does get harder to measure. This doesn't mean however that it can't be done or you shouldn't even try.

You know, or should know, what you have to achieve to keep the organisation in business. Work out with individuals what they need to do to help that. Give them the freedom to set their targets and get on with it – with your input of course. Or let the teams set their targets. People want to do a good job so let them.

Okay, this will take a good deal of time at the outset, but at least you're going in the right direction.

Alongside these objectives, you need to set the standard for how people behave. Again you need to involve people – what do they expect of you and their colleagues? It won't be a surprise to see everyone having the same views – supportive teamwork, effective communication, producing quality products and so on. Have a set of behaviours that people agree with and reward people who display those behaviours. You'll know who they are, your team will know how they are.

At the end of the year, you may want something in writing on how individuals have performed. You can be creative and ask your staff to write their own reports. They know how well they've done throughout the year. Again, I hear that little voice saying, *'But they'd give themselves top marks?'*

But would they? Would you? Of course not. You'd be harder on yourself than any manager.

Which is not to say that the manager has no role in this. They have an opinion as well, and they have the final decision – it's delegation not abdication. They will have their own standards and it's important they these are applied across the whole team.

This is not to say that you don't get much feedback on your performance throughout the year. You should gets a lot – constantly, not once in September and once in March. Ideally you get to have 360 degree feedback on your performance. You get feedback on how you can perform better. This isn't an appraisal – try to separate evaluation from development. People are more likely to give honest feedback if they feel it will be used for developmental purposes rather than as a stick to beat someone with. Correctly managed, the 360 degree feedback is a superb tool for doing this. However it needs to be extremely well managed. It's not an opportunity to settle scores, show off or make the other feel bad. It is a chance to help them. You will need to act as a sensitive facilitator in this. Look for the patterns. If one person out of the twelve gives incredibly harsh feedback in all areas, this may be a hint that there may be a personality clash more than anything else. So handle it sensitively. If you can't acknowledge it, get someone else to do it.

So, if you can't abolish performance management, you can at least make it a useful tool. Be honest, involve people and be creative.

'You receive from the world what you give to the world.'

Gary Zukav

Never, ever, negotiate with blackmailers, hostage takers or children, or so I've been told. Everything else is fair game then, I guess.

As a manager, you spend a great deal of your time negotiating. But do you or your staff get the best out of it? Do you negotiate consistently, or will one thing work for some staff one day but not the following day? Let's look at some ways to get a consistent approach to this tricky, subjective skill of negotiation.

The first thing to get clear is that you're not aiming for a 'I won – you lost' situation at all. Really you're not. Stephen Covey says that there are a number of outcomes to any negotiation;

- I lose – you lose
- I lose – you win
- I win – you lose
- I win – you win
- No deal

Okay, so let's take a look at these.

I lose – you lose. You'd need to be a masochist to gain any pleasure from this – a definite no.

I lose – you win. No thanks.

I win – you lose. As seductive as this sounds, this isn't a successful outcome to a negotiation. You win by making the other party lose. This may work in the short term but it's no long-term strategy. For instance, you've negotiated the cheapest deal to buy components from a small company. They've lost – you know they can't afford to make them at this price, but hey, that's not your problem. Is it? Well, I think it's going to become your problem in a few months time when they go bust and leave you desperately looking for a new supplier. You've got to work with these people, so keep relations friendly – who knows when you'll have to work with these people again.

I win – you win. Yes. Perfect – we've both got a deal we can work with.

No deal. If there's no possibility of reaching an agreement, stop it. Don't keep going for the sake of it – cut your losses and walk away before you sour relationships.

A useful model for helping work out if there's a 'no deal' scenario is The Negotiating Arena.

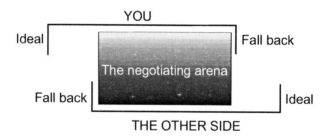

You have determined your Ideal position and your Fall Back position as has the person you are negotiating with. By doing this you can tell if there's any overlap. If there's not, just save some time and walk away. For example; I'd like to buy a car. Ideally I'd want to get it for free, but I'd be willing to pay up to £1,000. The car dealer has a car and ideally he'd like to sell it for £2,000 but would settle for £800. We have a negotiating arena.

The real benefit of this is that you can tell if there's no point negotiating. The downside to this is that it's too simple. Life's not really like this, is it? Would you go along to a car dealer and say *'Hello. I like that car and although I'd like you to give it me for nothing, I guess that's pretty unlikely, so I'd be willing to spend up to £1000.'*

'Well, thank you, sir, for being so honest. So, although I'd like the price on the window – £2,000 – for it, I know that's not going to happen so I would be willing to accept £800. Let's split the difference and if you give me £900, I'll give you the keys. Thanks. Have a nice day.'

Sound familiar? No. Also, there's rarely just the one factor involved in any negotiation. There is usually a whole host of conditions, options, offers and counter-offers. One of the key skills involved is in recognising these and using them effectively. The real challenge comes in the preparation. Do the homework and communicate.

This homework involves looking at your ideal and final offer for a range of conditions. Let's look at a simple example to get some ideas. You need your staff to send out some urgent work within the next two weeks or so. This work is extra – it's above and beyond their contracts and would involve working extra hours.

Look at as many options as you can think of and decide your ideal position and final offer for each, plus have some idea of the possible combinations. Some options may be – paid overtime, time off later, bringing in more staff. For each of these you'll have your ideals and final offer, e.g. overtime – ideally not, but you have a contingency of £2,000 if necessary.

So, having established this, you can begin the negotiation process. Think about the team. What do you know about their attitude to overtime, leave, outside recruitment? If it's possible, check this out. Look at past precedents. It'll give you some idea.

Then negotiate. Ideally, involve all of them and explain the problem and ask for suggestions. They may have some creative, constructive ideas that would work – rescheduling perhaps. Listen. Pick up any concerns. Check out the facts and discuss your ideas. Make requests, discuss and listen until you get to a win/win situation.

It's important here that you appreciate the difference between a request and a demand. A request can be accepted, declined or may produce a counter-request. Requests are healthy. Remember though that a request is a request – people can say no and you shouldn't get annoyed. If you are, then you're getting into making demands.

Demands are dangerous. People tend not to like demands – goes with the territory of blackmailers and hostage-takers. If people feel you are denying them a choice this will produce a reactant. This will tend to make them even more determined to do what you didn't want them to do anyway.

Tell a five year old to eat his vegetables and as soon as the words come out of your mouth, you know it's not going to happen. Make requests. There's no guarantee it'll happen but the odds suddenly get a lot better. In a work situation, threaten to withdraw overtime and suddenly you've got everyone working overtime even though they hadn't wanted to work overtime for years. Okay, I know what you're thinking, tell them not to do something you really want them to do. Theory sounds okay but that's manipulation. Once they realise they're working overtime because you've finessed them into doing it, that'll be the end of any happy working relationship.

Keep these basic principles for all negotiations – with your bank manager, your boss, your staff. Negotiation needn't be a process of hiding information and mistrust. Be open. Who knows – this approach could even work with blackmailers and hostage takers. Children? I seriously doubt it.

Making Hard Decisions
The joy of being a manager

'People they ain't no good.'

Nick Cave

You're a good manager. Two of your team are away from work on sick leave. This has put a great deal of pressure on the others. One of the others has asked for two days' leave starting tomorrow. What do you say?

The only answer of course is, *'Yes, of course you can. Is there anything else I can do to help?'*

You're a good manager – you communicate effectively. Your team are well motivated and know the current difficult situation you are in. So, if one of your team asks for time off in this situation, then you know it's important to them.

Anyway, what options have you got? You could say 'no' and then what would happen? At best you'd have a poorly motivated individual that would affect the team, who are under pressure enough, and would be thinking 'What if it were me that wanted time off?' This is the best scenario – she may not even turn up and you're left with another staff member short and no contingency plans.

What else could you do? Ask? Why would you? You're a good manager – you know your team – they know you. If they wanted to tell you – they'd tell you of their own volition, not because you ask. It may well be personal, it could be sensitive. Just assure her that you're there to listen and help if she needs it. You'd be much better spending your time looking for alternate ways to cover the work. Or better still, call all the staff together and ask them for ideas. They may be able to re-prioritise the work. They are the best ones to deal with it, after all, they're the ones who've got to do the work.

So why doesn't this feel particularly comfortable for a great many managers? Maybe they see management as a macho affair, and need

89

to be seen to be tough. Or, more charitably, they've been promoted into management for behaving in a certain way. They've been rewarded for getting results by themselves. Now, they're being told to behave differently. They now have to get results from others. Suddenly the control has shifted to the staff and they're thinking, *'This can't be right. I thought when I became manager I'd have more control – not less.'*. This can be incredibly frustrating. It's hardly surprising that it takes a while for managers to 'let go' of their previous jobs. The tendency is to do the new job and keep checking the old job. To me, this seems to be where the macho 'I've worked 60 hours this week' attitude starts.

A senior statistician once told me his management story.

'I was good at adding up sums so they promoted me. They gave me harder sums to do. I did this really well so they promoted me. They gave me even harder sums to do. I did this really well and they promoted me again. They moved me away from the sums and gave me fifty people to manage.'

I guess that's the story in a number of large organisations. Managers get rewarded for producing results, then get moved. You wouldn't do that with any other job would you? If an air hostess was excellent you wouldn't promote her to flying the plane would you? Or let a brilliant hospital porter perform a heart operation? When people become managers they need a different set of skills. This is frequently forgotten. In many organisations, someone can go home on the Friday having finished his shift on the production line, and come in on Monday responsible for fifty staff, having received no training at all. It's not surprising they feel under pressure or treat people the way they've been treated by previous managers – either well or badly.

This goes back to the 1960s. In 1960 Douglas McGregor published *The Human Side of Enterprise* that dealt with the management phenomenon he called theory X and theory Y. He established that there are two styles of management based on managers' own attitudes or assumptions.

Theory X states that managers believe that people hate work and will avoid it whenever possible, must be threatened with punishment to get anything out of them and are self-centred, resistant to change and basically not very bright.

Whereas there is another set of managers who he termed Theory Y managers who thought people regarded work as important and wanted to do a good job, are committed to organisations when they are offered suitable rewards, actively seek responsibility, have a great deal of imagination and creativity they are desperate to use in work, but unfortunately rarely realise their own potential at work.

According to McGregor, **Theory Y** managers tend to be the most successful, especially in the longer term as they produced better and more profitable results, had higher output and less waste, managed people who were more creative and had less staff turnover. Whereas the theory X manager tended to produce a blame and fear culture. The manager tended to interfere, get short-term results by bullying and created a very unhappy workforce with high turnover.

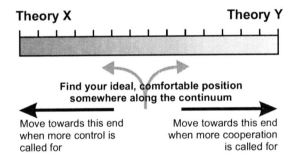

D McGregor's Continuum

There are a few role models for the Theory Y management style. For instance, managers like Ricardo Semler from Semco allowed his staff to have a say in choosing their manager and created a truly democratic workplace where staff were able to decide their own hours, their own pay.

Theory X type managers generally come from high pressure, results-driven areas. Most chefs would adopt the type X management style. A great many sales managers follow this approach. This isn't saying that they are bad people. People tend to behave in the way they've been treated. They see others having some success with this method and they assume there's no alternative. They may even feel that they've suffered in the hands of a type X manager so now it's their turn. There is an alternative.

The alternative, the theory Y type manager is not the soft option. This approach needs a very mature, grown up approach. To build trust and confidence in your team, you've got to allow them to try things. When they try things, they'll make mistakes. You've got to help them learn from those mistakes and move on. This can be incredibly frustrating – especially when you know what they should do. Ultimately you need the self belief that you're doing the right thing. If the team succeeds, they get the credit. If the team fails, you get the blame.

There are organisations that are 'theory X' organisations, where staff need to account for every minute of their time, and are searched on their way out. I've worked in an organisation where I needed senior management authority to get some urgent photocopying done. Imagine how you feel in that organisation. The message from the organisation is 'We don't trust you'.

If you walk into an office and see a rota chart, odds are you're looking at a theory X organisation. I've worked in teams where the very idea of a system telling people who was responsible for covering the phones would be laughed at. People knew what to do – knew they had to cover the phones and reception at certain times, so we did. The manager left us alone to sort it out. I firmly believe that people are pretty much like us – they're fundamentally good and they want to do a good job. If they're not behaving this way, then it'll be because they've been treated badly in the past and haven't learnt from it. All they need is for their managers to talk to them, show some trust and respect and let them prove themselves.

I know there are times when the theory X approach works – there are chefs, generals that get results by this fear approach. But it's short-term winning only. I know who I'd want to work for, especially if I wanted two days leave for personal reasons.

<table>
<tr><td>

**TECHNIQUE
NO 21**

</td><td>

Getting Out of the Comfort Zone and Looking Closely at Some Barriers

</td></tr>
</table>

'Only those who dare to fail greatly can ever achieve greatly.'
Robert F Kennedy

If you're working for an organisation you don't own, stop for a moment and think. If this were your organisation would you do anything differently?

Consider this scenario – you and some colleagues do the lottery and win £14 million and decide to buy your organisation. What would you change? Now what would you do differently? If you haven't got lots of ideas, I'm sure your staff will have. Ask them.

So what's stopping you making those changes? I guess there are a number of difficulties. I guess you can see a lot of problems that will stop you doing things the way you'd like to.

The difficulty with problems is that they all look insoluble until you've solved them. There is, to the solver, absolutely no difference between an impossible problem and a problem you haven't yet solved.

For instance try this.

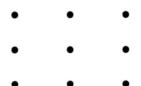

Here are 9 dots arranged in a square. Without taking your pencil off the paper, draw four straight lines to connect all the dots (answer below).

What did you feel like while you're doing this? I guess it's frustration, anger, annoyance, maybe you even gave up. You go through the same range of emotions you go through when you go through some change process. Believe it or not this is a good place to be- 'If you're not churning, you're not learning'.

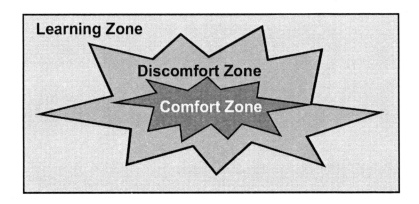

To really learn something important, you have to go through some discomfort. The degree of discomfort you go through depends on a whole range of factors; you, the task, the importance, coaching and support, etc. But you do need to go through the discomfort zone to reach the learning zone. There is no magic tunnel that will take you from the comfort zone to the learning zone. There are a number of factors that will make the discomfort zone less traumatic but you still need to get through it. A learning environment and confidence in yourself will help. However, even those who love learning and have a supportive network still need to take that step.

For instance you can learn Welsh in a nice pleasant room, with lots of books, CDs, help and support and you think you've got this learning thing sorted. However it's only when you get to Aberystwyth and try to ask for directions do you know if it'll work or not.

People will try to sell you anything to get you over the discomfort zone – learn a foreign language while you sleep – learn to stop smoking by listening to this tape, trying these patches, hypnosis. Do they work? I don't think so. You've got to get through that discomfort. Remember learning to drive? Enough said.

So you know you're in a good place because it's uncomfortable – you're churning, you're learning so let's look at the problems, the barriers.

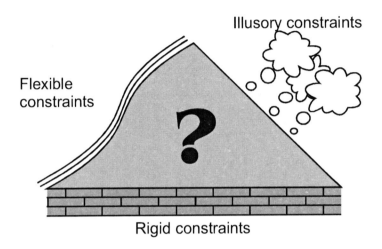

The first types of barriers are the solid barriers – **rigid constraints**, these are real. There's not enough money to hire someone else – the law won't allow us to trade that way. Look at these barriers carefully – can you do anything to control or influence them in any way? If you can, then do it. It'll be a start. Legislation can be changed – it takes time but it does happen.

There may be different ways of looking at the problem. Okay, the budget is such that you can't hire another person. What are the alternatives? Change something – drop something – re-prioritise. If you've tried everything and still can't get around it – then drop it. Totally. It will drain you if it's on the bottom of a 'to do' list. Incompletions drain energy, completions give you energy. This has been proven physically, not just mentally. If you have 'to do' lists, include a number of small manageable tasks amongst the big jobs so that when you're feeling down and tired of the big tasks, you can complete a small one. Then cross it out. This will give you a rush of energy, endorphins are released.

The next type of barriers are the **flexible constraints**. These are real barriers but often they're not as solid as they appear. Frequently they only need a different perspective.

For instance, when Walt Disney was building Disney world in Orlando, Florida, it looked to be a near impossible task. Imagine trying to build anything that solid on what was basically swamp land. The first thing he built was the huge castle. This was, architecturally, not the best option but as a statement of intent and a vision, it was absolutely perfect. It was inspirational to all the staff.

Marks and Spencers had a problem with their sandwiches in their food stores. They found that it was taking so much effort to butter them that the cost would be too high. Martin van Zwanenberg realised that *'if we wanted to expand, this was unacceptable – we'd have to have everyone in the company buttering bread.'* So he approached it in a different way. He had seen silk-screen printing and decided to try that approach. *'We filled up one of the ink vats with butter and screen-printed butter onto bread'*. It was a great success at a fraction of the price.

Hewlett-Packard's approach had always been, as most product-based services had been, to build a product then sell it. This was causing problems with supply chains so they decided to implement a policy of selling the computer first then building it. This gives them greater flexibility; *'We still build something different, but equally good if a supplier lets us down. This flexibility also helps a customer like Wal-Mart because they get the best machine we can make for the price and get it on time'*, said Corey Billington. They proved they could produce better quality, cheaper machines than previously by looking at the problem in a different way.

Then there are the barriers that only existing our heads, or in the heads of people in the organisation. These are **illusory constraints**. You suggest something that seems perfectly sensible.
> *'So, we just don't hold the meeting as we've nothing to talk about.'*
> *'But we've got to.'*

'Why?'

'The coffee's already been ordered.'

Or *'We've always done it that way!'*

Some great quick wins have been carried out by new leaders challenging this status quo. For example – John Harvey Jones started holding meetings in offices instead of boardrooms. Ricardo Semler ordered security to stop searching employees as they left the premises.

These are problems that can be solved quickly – with just a mind shift. New people are great at seeing this.

'So, why do you do that?' they may say. These are the real 'open goals' – they cost little but often achieve a great deal. In an organisation I worked with, in my computer programmer days, a new trainee asked why we kept all the computer reports each day, then moved them the next day, stored them for a week then threw them away.

'Because we do.'

'Do you ever use them?

'Well we could use them if there were a problem.'

'So when was the last time you had a problem?'

'Last week.'

'And did you use them?'

'Of course not. You'd never find anything. We have all the information on screen. It's so much easier to find.'

It was estimated that this saved £20,000 a year in paper, workload, storage etc.

There was a Personal Assistant on a training course with me who became very upset about the communications session we were running. Talking to her, I found that she had been upset for months about her office. She wanted to move her desk so that she faced the door. She knew her boss extremely well and knew he hated change, he liked everything to be 'just so' and would not be pleased. Throughout the week we did some coaching with the PA and devised a strategy of a conversation she could have with her manager. She had five or six excellent reasons and had worked out some benefits for him. We had rehearsed the situation a few times with me taking on his role and acting as I thought he would. By the end of the week she was determined – she would see him Monday and call to let me know how it went. She was still incredibly nervous but determined.

She called Monday. *'I came to work early, practised what I was going to say, kept breathing and waited. He came in at 9 o'clock, as always and I took a deep breath and asked him if I could move the desk because ... He stopped me. "Yes, of course," he said and went for his coffee leaving me with a whole 20-minute rehearsed speech and no-one to tell it to.'*

So, if it were your own business – what would you do differently?

Answer to dots problem:

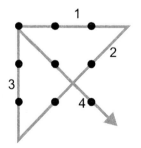

Is this where 'thinking outside the box' came from?

'Gonna change my way of thinking,
Make myself a different set of rules.
Gonna change my way of thinking,
Make myself a different set of rules.
Gonna put my good foot forward,
And stop being influenced by fools.'

B Dylan

I once heard Robert Holden, management consultant, at a seminar describing a consultancy session he carried out for some BBC executives involving change and the management of change.

All the senior executives at the BBC were sitting in a semicircle. He asked them to stand up and change seats – they did. Then he asked them to change seats again – they did, and again, and again, and again. After about twenty minutes one of them said, *'What are you doing this for?'*

'It's only what you've been doing to your staff for the past twelve months,' came the reply.

Change is uncomfortable. Most people dislike change intensely. You don't believe me – look around – people tend to stay in the same places, for work, in meetings, for lunch, on the bus home, in the pub. People don't like change.

It's so easy to say this though, isn't it? Why this happens may be more useful. I heard Michael Palin on a TV chat show once talking about his childhood, and in particular his first five years. He thought the world was a bit of a fuzzy place. It was only when he had his eyes tested and had glasses that he realised it wasn't. It was a quite focused place. Perhaps this is one reason people aren't keen on change – conditioning. People will tend to accept things as they are. With change, people may not be fighting it or going along with it at the

99

beginning because they may be unaware that it's happening.

There was a set of experiments carried out by Stanley Milgram in the 1960s, looking at conformity and obedience. In one typical experiment subjects were asked to administer electric shocks to 'learners' if these learners made a mistake in order to help them learn more effectively. There were no real electric shocks given. Each time the learners made a mistake the voltage was increased and the learners (actors) feigned discomfort and then pain. As the voltage reached (what the subjects thought) were dangerous levels, they asked to stop. The experimenters asks them to continue and invariably they did, even though they believed they were harming people. In the first set of experiments, 65% of people carried on until the final '450 volts'.

There have been a number of reasons put forward to explain this behaviour and one of the more powerful is people's willingness to obey authority and to resist change. At some level, that happens to many of us faced with actively avoiding change. In terms of conformity within teams, Solomon Asch carried out experiments in which a subject was placed with a group of 'confederates' and all were asked to announce their judgement to the length of several lines drawn on displays. When some lines were shown, they were asked which was the smallest, largest and so on. The confederates had been asked to give the incorrect answers.

Although many of the subjects felt uneasy, the vast majority of them conformed and gave the same incorrect answers as the others. This would appear to be an undeniable example of the potential danger of 'group think' and the effects peer pressure can have on individuals. It makes it even more clear that when managing change, managers have to be incredibly clear about the pressures individuals have on them to resist. Apart from these examples of conformity, once people realise that change is happening, there's the fear of the unknown, fear of loss of power, loss of self-esteem, loss of self respect to deal with as well. All perfectly rational fears for individuals caught up in the process.

People have to realise that something is happening before you can help them. They need to be aware – so let them know.

It's not only individuals, but often organisations that need to be dragged kicking and screaming through change. This could be technological change, social change or perhaps a change in the vision of new leaders. Many organisations resist and go under. For example, Encyclopaedia Britannica didn't respond quickly enough to the change in technology from books to computers – and failed.

Change can often be very uncomfortable ... Try this.

You've an ordinary round cake in front of you and you have a knife. What is the maximum number of pieces you can produce with just 3 cuts? Cuts have to be straight. Can you get 6, 7, 8, 9?

Okay, I don't think 9 is possible (unless you start cutting at strange vertical and horizontal angles) but six is okay and straightforward, cutting the cake into equal slices. Seven looks like this.

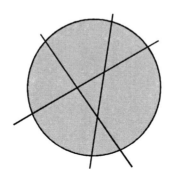

Eight consists of two vertical cuts and then a horizontal cut through the cake.

So, what emotions were you going through during this? (unless you've seen this before – or got it first time?) I guess it's not comfortable. If you're in a room with others it will be worse. Typical reactions are that people feel stupid, embarrassed, angry, resentful, blameful. I've seen a few people walking out muttering, 'stupid trainer games'. Frequently people just give up.

This will be because change is uncomfortable. All change or

learning involves discomfort. People go through a number of emotional stages when dealing with change. This can be illustrated in a model originally devised by Adams, Hayes and Hopson called the Coping Cycle. In management terms, it's vital to appreciate that people are at different stages in terms of change.

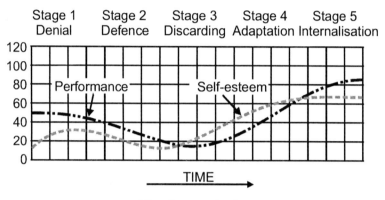

The Coping Cycle

This is a good model to describe the emotions and feelings people often go through during change or learning. For me, a good definition of learning is that you can do something now you couldn't do before. You have changed. From giving up smoking to merging two organisations – this model seems to work. The time people spend in each zone varies considerably depending on the intensity of the change and the person's ability to deal with it. Some people never get to the end of this cycle. Walking around the office, you see people stuck in **denial/defence** from years ago.

'I still make a hand written copy.'
'Why?'
'In case the computer crashes – it did once in 1994.'
'But the data's backed up and this takes you hours.'
'Ah well, you can't be too careful.'

As a manager, how does this help? The key is the 3Cs - communicate, communicate, communicate. Tell people what's going on. The best change programmes have regular updates even when there's nothing to report. It lets people know that it hasn't gone away and you haven't forgotten to tell them anything. There's just no news.

I remember the Performance Management System we had in one organisation I worked at. It was hated. On every training course, it would be mentioned – too long, too unwieldy, a complete waste of time. The following year there was a complete change and the system was totally revamped. My task was to introduce it to the staff in nice, easy half-day sessions with 30 or so staff each time. After a few days, I felt battered.

'Why can't we go back to the old system,' they said, *'it was great.'*

Suddenly there was a change coming along and they were desperate to get the old system working properly. People were stuck in the defence and denial stages. At these stages, things frequently work better initially. That old system that never worked properly starts to improve as people spend more effort trying to make it work. There are many stories of people in defence and denial mode. My favourite was from a colleague who was a tax inspector in Wales – he used to go around West Wales inspecting betting shops and ensuring they had paid the correct amount of tax.

One day in 1976 he was working way up the Swansea valley visiting a small village (well more like a wide spot in the road) called Abercwmtoch – a few houses, 2 pubs, a church and a betting office. In the betting office he looks through the tickets and sees all sort of strange things; 2 shilling each way bets, 6d wins, 2/6 yankee. Bearing in mind this is 1976 – 5 years after decimalisation. It hasn't quite reached Abercwmtoch yet.

'Ah, that new fangled decimalisation,' you can hear them saying. *'It'll never catch on.'*

I wonder if they've changed now.

So, people tend to resist change. So help them, explain why, explain the benefits, the problems. Stage three in this process is called **discarding**. This is where the change is happening and the old ways are going. This is progress and you have to keep reminding them that it is progress, because it may not feel like it. To move forward, they need to let go. This feels bad and frequently things get worse before they get better.

When I worked in a computer department, they introduced a new email system with little help at all – we were IT, we were supposed to be the clever ones. I could not see it at all. I was so much slower than I'd been with the old system for days. What did I do? Did I do the sensible thing and ask for help? Of course not, like most people, we've our pride, so I started coming into the office early and staying late until I got the hang of it.

How much better it would have been to have someone talk to me. Explain that it would slow me down initially but eventually it would have great benefits (it did). Try to remember what you felt like confronted with something new and show some empathy.

The final stages of **adaptation** and **internalisation** are far more positive. Things are beginning to go well again. People can see the benefits and have stopped fighting. Keep communicating and rewarding people. These are the stages where people say things like *'I don't know why we didn't do this sooner. It's a great Performance Management System/email system/currency.'*

Sometimes the change fails for a simple reason – more change comes on top of it. It seems to be a factor these days that there's change overload or 'hyper change overload' to coin a current phrase. The problem with this is that as soon as one change is introduced the next one kicks in.

Kurt Lewin has a simple three step model that can help this process.

It involves scheduling time for this vital 'bedding in' stage. The three stages are **unfreezing, moving** or **changing** and **refreezing**. Imagine the change process as a block of ice. The first action is to melt it so that you can begin working on it. The next stage involves changing it. Changing the behaviours and attitudes of the people involved. The final stage involves refreezing and establishing these new behaviours and attitudes as standard before you change again. Too frequently, this last stage gets shortened, or missed out totally, whilst the next initiative kicks in – leaving a lot of frustrated, unhappy staff.

So there are a number of models to help. All of them seem to have the same message – talk to your people and let them know what's happening. Organisations need to change to move forward and if you're not moving forward, you're likely not to be surviving for much longer. As the title of Robert Holden's book says *'Shift happens'*.

<table>
<tr><td>

**TECHNIQUE
NO 23**

</td><td>

Coaching and Building
Relationships

</td></tr>
</table>

'90% of the game is half mental.'

Yogi Beera

Coaching is as much a part of the day to day life in an office as ... arguing whose turn it is to collect the lottery money. I bet it is. I guess there's a lot more coaching goes on in offices than we'd like to admit.

'How do I attach a photo to an email?' – coaching.
'Quick – give me some idea of what I've got to say at this meeting.' – coaching.
'Over the next few months, we'll work together on the strategic plan.' – coaching.
'How the hell does this kettle work?' – coaching.

Coaching covers the whole spectrum of training and development skills from instructing at the one end to counselling at the other end. The skilful coach moves along this spectrum using the most appropriate methods for each situation.

There are a number of skills, tools and techniques managers should have in their back pockets to help. The first, and the most important, is to recognise the importance of coaching. It's not just a vehicle for passing on knowledge. It's a great way of building relationships, motivating and finding out what's happening with your staff. Once you understand that, you will be actively looking for coaching opportunities as a chance to manage your staff more effectively. All you need do now is to spot the opening.

The quality of any management activity such as coaching is directly related to the quality of the relationship between the manager and member of staff. Build a strong relationship and you'll be a better, more effective coach and manager. This will, of course, also apply to the strength of the relationships within that team. You've worked in teams where you've really gelled with people and there's a buzz. I guess you've also worked with people, who may even have been more competent, but there just wasn't that chemistry. You know which one you'd prefer to work again, don't you?

In practical terms, coaching is a perfect way to build relationships. Another vital aspect is talking to your people every day. As you come into the office, do you talk to all your staff? This may sound obvious or not important but I've been in teams where the boss didn't do this, for very good reasons – she was frequently busy and permanently shy, and it was hell for her. It led to an 'us and them' attitude which was not helpful to anyone.

Another, more formal approach is to go away with your team for the day and get them to complete a sociometric test. This consists of the following diagram, where each member of the team has a sheet of paper with his or her name at the centre and the names of the other team members arranged around them.

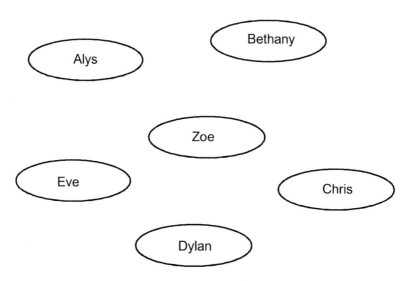

Each person has to indicate the strength of their working relationship with each other member of the team. This is done by drawing a line from them to each member with the thickness of the line representing the relationship. So, as in Zoe's diagram below a thick line as Alys-Zoe indicates a very strong working relationship, whilst a dotted line Dylan – Zoe indicates a weak working relationship.

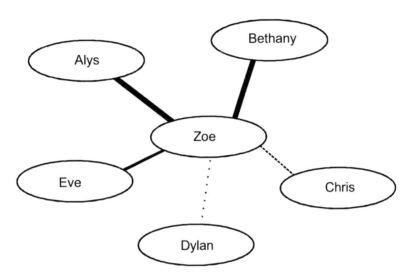

Now you arrange each pair to get together in a quiet space and talk about their perceptions. If there are weak links, they may consider strengthening them, or if they are too strong, weakening them. If they are a very mature team, you could even map all the links on a master chart and look at the overall picture.

This can be an extremely powerful exercise and, if you are willing to do it, you must be totally comfortable with it and what it could bring out. It may bring out some tensions and unhappiness. That unhappiness however is there anyway, and no one's talking about it. One other point – keep emphasising that it is about working relationships.

So, back to the coaching ... someone has a difficulty.

'Which button do I press?'

You look at the screen. *'Control and F8'.*

Job done? Well not really. Tomorrow, you'll get the same question and the day after and the day after. Stop. Take some time and explain what to do and why you're doing it. This will take more time in the short term but trust me – it'll save so much time in the long run. It'll save time and seriously reduce the risk of the individual pressing the wrong button because he or she is too embarrassed to ask again. It'll also help building that relationship.

As a general rule, don't solve people's problems for them. There will be some exceptions that we'll look at later, but if you possibly can, let them figure it out. This is definitely the best approach. Honestly. Well, you tell me what'll happen if someone comes to you with a problem and you solve it perfectly? They'll be pleased, yes. You'll feel pleased with yourself as well, yes. However the next time they have a problem, they'll be back knocking on your door asking for more advice.

What if you get it wrong? They'll be back again, but this time just the once and possibly not very pleased either. If you've suggested they sell the children, move out, put all their savings on a horse and turn vegetarian and this isn't the correct solution, they may not be too happy. You can't win. What you can do is to *help them help themselves*. Coach or counsel them.

One very useful technique is known as SPIN. This is a technique that can be used for good or evil so be careful. It is frequently used in the field of sales and can be manipulative. It is a process using four types of questions, used systematically. These are **Situation** questions, **Problem** questions, **Implication** questions, and **Needs** questions.

For example, you've decided you want to buy a kitchen. You plan to visit a few showrooms, get a few ideas, a few quotes and go home to think about it. An hour later, you find yourself buying a kitchen from the first showroom you visited that you're not sure you need and not even convinced you can afford. How did that happen? Well you may have been 'spun'.

The salesperson asks, *'How are you?'*

'Fine,' you reply, *'just looking.'*

'Okay – if you need any help, I'll be right here.'

So far so good – *Situation* questions – nice and friendly just to establish a rapport.

'*So,*' the salesperson says, '*is it a kitchen or a bathroom you're interested in?*'

'*Kitchen.*'

'*I see, so what are you after? What's your current kitchen like?*'

They ask *problem* questions, listening intently for clues.

You tell them it's too old/too modern/difficult to clean/too big/too small.

They hone in on the problem.

'*So, what'll happen if you don't get a replacement?*'

'*So, you can't get all your shopping in the cupboards when you come home?*'

These *implication* questions are used to get you to recognise the significance of the problem.

Now you're hooked.

Then the *needs* questions. '*So, what would be ideal for you is a kitchen with a more traditional feel?*'

'*So, you'd really appreciate a kitchen like this that requires hardly any cleaning?*'

… and then, '*Luckily, I've got just the thing for you – this kitchen is new/traditional/easy to clean/compact/huge.*'

It will be more subtle than that, but it can often have the same result. Intrinsically, it's not a bad approach at all. Let's look at your problem and help solve it. It can be manipulative however when the salesperson has decided beforehand that you're having this kitchen with the biggest mark-up whatever your need is.

In coaching terms, it's the same approach. Use nice, open, settling questions. Then start them talking about problems. '*What difficulties have you found so far?*' Then start closing them down to specifics – '*So what will happen if that's not sorted immediately?*' Then the major change in emphasise. '*What do you need to do to address that?*' They can ask for your help but the problem (and solution) is theirs. They need to own it. Then you give them space to decide how they're going to move this forward.

There is a misconception that to coach someone effectively in a task you need to be able to be an expert in that task. Not necessarily so. You need to be able to coach skilfully and I admit it does help if you have some idea of the subject,. However experts can frequently get it wrong by getting the level of help wrong. They are frequently so expert at their subject that that find it impossible to approach it from the level of a complete beginner. They assume things. Good coaches don't.

The skills of coaching are different from the skills of doing, otherwise Tiger Woods' coach would be beating Tiger Woods. Coaching is a matter of demonstrating basic management and people skills – communication, showing empathy, giving feedback skilfully, being non-judgmental. It's a matter of being a good manager basically.

<table>
<tr><td>

TECHNIQUE NO 24
</td><td>

Meetings - Some Purely Practical Approaches
</td></tr>
</table>

'How I dearly wish I was not here
In the seaside town
... that they forgot to bomb
Come, come, come – nuclear bomb.'

SP Morrissey

A new definition of a meeting:

A gathering of essential participants only, each of whom has something to contribute, to discuss a problem touching on all their interests, to arrive at certain decisions, all as required by the predetermined aim of the meeting itself.

David Martin

If possible – don't go. Unless someone can convince you that there is a real purpose and that you are the best person to go – refuse to go.

There are thousands of meetings held every day. Many of them, as you know, are at best, worthless, and at worst, demotivating and a total waste of time. There are a number of alternatives to meetings – explore all of these first before you call a meeting;

So you think you want to hold a meeting? Ask yourself – could you possibly do something else, could you email people the information, could you talk on the phone? Could *you* decide on an action and let people know? If none of these options works, ask yourself:

- Why are you holding a meeting?
- What is the purpose of the meeting and what is the intended result?

If you can't answer those two basic questions, there's no benefit to holding a meeting. If you're asked to attend a meeting and the person setting up the meeting can't tell you the purpose and intended result - you'll be wasting your time.

Ask yourself – do I really need this meeting? Can I just decide what I want to do and then let others know? Am I trying to shift responsibility? If you are in a position to decide without holding a meeting – decide.(Remember it is easier to ask for forgiveness than permission). If you're concerned, then phone or email others telling them what you intend to do and asking them if they have any objections.

Information

If the meeting is merely to pass on information, can you do this in another way? Can you send a report, a video of a presentation, a link? If you can, do it and allow people time to digest this information at their own time do.

If you decide you really have to have a meeting, there are a few questions to think about carefully;

Who should attend?

Don't invite people to a meeting because they always come to these meetings. If you know people are only attending because of their position in the organisation, investigate it. The number of managers who rush to junior members of staff before a meeting to be briefed and then have to brief them after the meeting must be phenomenal. Get the right person to attend – irrespective of his or her position.

People often don't need to stay around for the entire meeting. Prepare an agenda of who should stay or go, for each item on the agenda. There is nothing worse than sitting through a three-hour meeting waiting for your ten-minute slot at the end that will invariably be postponed until the next time because the meeting has run out of time.

Using time

That's another thing – time. This is maybe the key element. Be ruthless. Schedule an item and schedule a time. If there is an item that's so vital it has to be decided, hold a meeting for that one topic. For less dramatic meetings if an item is scheduled for 20 minutes and time's up and you're nowhere near a conclusion, stop it – reschedule it and move on to the next item. This will be incredibly hard to begin with but people will soon learn to get to the point quicker.

If possible, separate information sharing meetings from decision making meetings. Inevitably the person who has presented the information will have a bias towards getting it accepted even if there are stronger arguments. Separate these meetings – ideally over a day or so to allow people to assimilate all the information. Or at the very least take a break between the presentations and the voting.

Some alternatives

There are some different ways of holding meetings and different approaches that may not be popular with a few people early on but they will get used to it;

Stand-up meetings. No chairs, no coffee – a quick Monday morning progress meeting would be a good candidate. People are surprising eloquent and to the point once they've been standing for ten minutes or so.

Choose the most appropriate location. This doesn't necessarily mean the meeting room with comfortable seats. If it's your meeting, you choose.

Start exactly on time. If people are late, they get to miss it this time. It will encourage people to get used to your way of doing things.

Never, ever have Any Other Business – ever. If people can't inform you before the meeting, it can't be that important, or they are doing it for tactical reasons.

You can have creative meetings – really. They can be fun and extremely productive. If you have a problem, or a proposal to look at, try something a little different. One technique is to use the principles outlined in Edward de Bono's *'Six Thinking Hats'*.

The chair will have the blue hat, which manages the process. Other attendees are given a particular colour hat and must act out that particular colour;

- black hat is for negativity and why something won't work,
- white hat is concerned with information – facts and figures,
- red hat deals with feelings and intuition,
- yellow hat symbolises optimism and positive thinking
- green hat focuses on creativity.

So, once these roles are assigned, the topic is discussed. The black hat thinkers will look for reason this won't work. The white hat thinkers will argue on the basis of facts and figures, and so on. The discussions are usually lively and productive. People don't get trapped into defending positions but can explore ideas in a creative way. A similar approach may be for all to look at the problem with the black hat mentality, then all look at it from a creative angle, and so on. This does work. There are organisations that actually have different coloured hats that help.

Meetings needn't be that bad but you do have to control them. They do develop a life of their own once they occur regularly. People frequently go along to a project or group meeting way past its sell buy date. The last item should be 'Give me a Purpose and Intended Result for the next meeting, else it's not going to happen.' If someone can't, then there's no meeting.

<table>
<tr><td>

TECHNIQUE NO 25

</td><td>

Putting It All Together - Four Models to Remember

</td></tr>
</table>

'It's a funny thing, the more I practice the luckier I get.'
G Player

Management is one of those things that do get easier the more you do it, as long as you build the correct habits from the start. Keep going back to basics. These four models are basic, pragmatic and simple – perfect for managers.

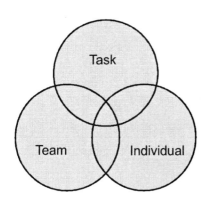

John Adair's Action Centred Leadership

If you need a screen saver to remind you how to be a great leader, I suggest this. I know it's not original but it really captures the three key areas to keep your eyes on. As a leader or manager, you need to get the job done (task), keep your staff motivated (team) and keep reminding yourself that your team is made up of people (individual).

It's useful to keep this in mind every day. It's so easy when you get trapped in a routine to forget and generally it's the team or the individual that suffer. There will be times when the task must take precedent but you need to re-establish the balance as soon as you can afterward.

If you ignore this you're heading for a disaster. In a large organisation I was involved with in the 1990s, this was a problem. This was at the stage that computing in large organisations really took off. There was a team of four who formed the computer support team. As the demands on the computer and the support team grew, the

117

numbers in that team stayed the same. What was once a well motivated, effective team with a long list of people waiting to join them seemed to disintegrate over a few months.

They became a team of three when one of the staff left for health reasons. He was not replaced and this meant the team were under more stress – more TASK TASK TASK. It took the threat of an overtime ban to force the managers to reappraise the situation and introduce another team of three.

If you concentrate on one aspect of the Adair model, the others will suffer. Usually the area is the task, but I have worked with teams where people are only concerned with their own individual development, or the focus is on keeping the team happy – and the results are equally as dramatic.

There are many, many ways of redressing the balance (This book is full of them). So, here's my top tips for redressing the balance in each area.

To look at the task in more detail it is useful to look at the amount of time you spend doing various activities. If you seem to be spending a great deal of your time fire-fighting, then maybe it's time for you to stop and work out why the fires start in the first place. The Stephen Covey model below is an excellent, and simple, way of looking at this.

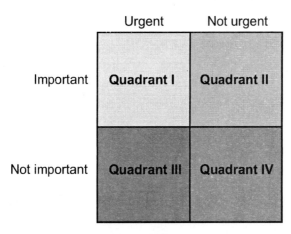

Stephen Covey – Time Management Grid

Have a look at your work patterns and try to establish how much time you are devoting to each quadrant. How much time do you spend in each part of the diagram?

Quadrant I activities *(urgent and important)* e.g. fire fighting, crises
Quadrant II activities *(not urgent and important)* e.g. relationship building, strategic thinking
Quadrant III activities *(urgent and not important)* e.g. interruptions, some meeting, more fire fighting
Quadrant IV activities *(not urgent and not important)* e.g. many meetings, lots of mail.

The key to freeing up time is to expand Quadrant II. It needs a different and brave approach. You need to find a way of freeing up time from the other quadrants. Quadrants III and IV may be easier than Quadrant I. However, if you are serious about changing this balance, you will need to do it. Things will never improve until you spend more time carrying out Quadrant II activities. If you can carry out more Quadrant II activities, you can spend more time thinking strategically, working out where the fires come from and how to put them out. It is an incredibly effective, simple tool that should save a great deal of effort and stress.

To help with the team there is an excellent model by Senge which deals with commitment from your team and how aligned they are to your goals. The big arrow in the diagram is the strategic direction of your organisation. The little arrows are the stakeholders, the people, the groups.

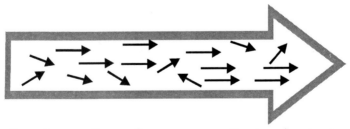

Peter Senge – Team alignment - non-effective organisation

Is this diagram representative of the direction your team are heading in? They could be the best group of individuals in the world but they're unlikely to get results unless they have an agreed goal. They need not have the same objectives but these objectives need to be complimentary for the team to succeed. Let me give you an example from football. Arsene Wenger (manager of Arsenal) will have an objective for his team to be the best in the world. It would be nice if all his players had the same objective. It would still work if Thierry Henry's aim was to be the best footballer in the world – not the same objective but complimentary. This would still involve teamwork, supporting others and so on. However, if his aim is to be the 'top goalscorer' this may not work as this could make problems within the team. Maybe he would never pass, never help the others.

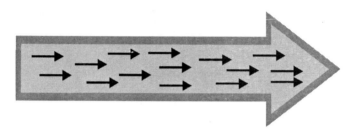

Peter Senge – Team alignment - effective organisation

The best and easiest way to get all your teams' arrows pointing in the direction you want them to go is to *communication your vision*. Tell them as clearly as possible where you want to go and keep telling them. If they have different goals, talk about it. It may be that by being the top salesperson in the organisation it will help you – that is fine. As long as the goals are not contradictory it will work. There's the quote from Bill Russell, Boston Celtics basketball coach: *'We were a team of specialists, and like a team of specialists in any field, our performance depended on both individual excellence and how well we worked together.'*

If you need to develop the individual, a useful model to look at is the **Johari Window**. The name isn't as romantic as it sounds as it was devised by Joe and Harry – Joseph Luft and Harry Ingham. It's a window with four panes and describes how individuals interact.

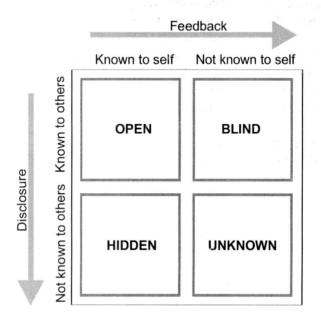

The Johari Window

In the **OPEN** pane is information about you that you know and others know – your name, your motivation, likes and dislikes, details that you choose to reveal (it's known to yourself and others). The 'openness' of an individual will affect how big this segment is.

The **BLIND** segment is the information others know about you that you don't know. This is peoples' impressions of you. How confident you appear, how expert you are and so on.

The **HIDDEN** area is that part that you know about yourself that others don't. This area is filled with your own perceptions, feelings about yourself – your insecurities, for example.

The final area is the **UNKNOWN**. This is an area of untapped potential that neither you nor others know about.

The learning from this is in opening up the open segment of this window. You can do this in two ways.

- You trust people more and start disclosing, which extends the open window into the hidden window.
- You ask for feedback and expand into the blind area.

Both these approaches will allow you to tap into the UNKNOWN area where there is a wealth of potential.

This may all seem very interesting. ' But so what?' I hear you say. This can be a very powerful mechanism for learning and individual change. A few personal examples may help.

I worked as a consultant working with specialist statisticians. I had a real problem with statisticians at the time. I put them on a pedestal and thought they were so incredibly clever it intimidated me. One in particular I was in awe of. He could carry out calculations in his head at lightening speed. We were on a five-day training course and after day one, I found it difficult to work with him. In the evening I was talking to some of his colleagues and decided to be open and disclose some of my concerns, so I did.

They looked at each other and started laughing. *'Great,'* I thought, *'They're laughing at me.'*

But they weren't.

'You've been intimidated by Mike?' they queried.

'Of course,' I replied. *'He's so quick.'*

'He's quick, okay, but he's always wrong. We never trust any of the figures from him.'

Another story comes from the time I was working as a computer programmer and was thinking about changing my job. I was just so bored. I was attending a management development course and the session was about the Johari window. Later, I talked to the trainer and told him that I was thinking of changing jobs and that I'd quite like to try training and consultancy. He told me that he'd noticed the way I'd been working through the week and that this would be an excellent move for me. We discussed this some more and two weeks later I joined the training team.

The disclosure and feedback does work. If you're willing to take that first step, the payoff can often be dramatic.

These models are excellent as long as you use them. They're simple, easy and very pragmatic. But you've got to keep going back to them. Keep practising and you'll be surprised what a luckier manager you become.